# HOME BUYING POWER

# HOME BUYING POWER

*The Savvy Shopper's Guide to Paying Less and Getting More in Any Real Estate Market*

MARTI KILBY

*This book is dedicated to all of the buyers who have trusted me to help them buy a place to call home. All of their experiences, the great and not-so-great, form the foundation for this book.*

*And a special thanks to my insanely talented husband, Ronn, who has tirelessly supported me in my real estate career. Whether I needed a logo design, a book cover, or cutting-edge video tours, he has been there for me every step of the way.*

# TABLE OF CONTENTS

# INTRODUCTION

Buying a home is probably the single largest purchase most people will make in their lifetime. It is a complicated process, and, unfortunately, we all know someone who's suffered from buyer's remorse. Maybe the home didn't really fit their needs, or the location was far from ideal. Perhaps they overpaid, or they bought a lemon that rapidly became a money pit. Whatever the story, the potential for costly and emotionally upsetting problems is what makes home buying so scary for many people.

That's about to change. This book will make you a savvy shopper; one who's less likely to purchase the wrong home and more likely to get the best possible deal for their money. I will take you step by step through the complete home-buying process—from determining if you are ready to buy; to financing, inspections, and negotiating; and finally to closing escrow and enjoying your new home. The book is written in chronological order, breaking the process down into chapters and identifying tips along the way that will save you money and improve your odds of getting the home you want. Of course, markets will vary according to local economies, but whether you're in a seller's or buyer's market, there are steps you can take to improve your bargaining position.

As a real estate broker and REALTOR®—and as the owner of a real estate company in San Diego County—I have helped countless buyers find and purchase the home that's right for them. It all comes down to gaining a better understanding of the process at each step, identifying your own needs versus wants, and learning some money-saving tips. As I operate in San Diego County, the items I discuss in this book are based on California law and practices, but all of the principles are generally applicable throughout the US.

At the end of the book, I've included a Glossary, but there are a few terms pertaining to real estate professionals that should be clarified up front. Every state requires that a person representing others in the buying or selling of real estate be licensed by the state in which they do business. Real estate *brokers* are licensed to act on their own—having met extensive educational requirements and passed a comprehensive exam—while licensed real estate *agents* or *salespersons* also must meet educational requirements and pass an exam, but they must act under the supervision of a broker. I also want to clarify the difference between a REALTOR and a real estate agent. A *REALTOR* is a member of the National Association of REALTORS (NAR), a trade organization devoted to supporting professionalism and ethics throughout the real estate industry. Each state also has an affiliated Association of REALTORS, as do most large cities. Not all agents, salespersons, or brokers are REALTORS, but in many parts of the country, NAR membership is regarded as a sign of commitment to the highest levels of professionalism. Although I use the term *real estate agent* to refer to the profession in general, I have written this guide with the standards of the National Association of REALTORS in mind. That being said, I hope that agents throughout the country will see this book as a helpful guide to share with their buyers. I have tremendous respect for my fellow professionals, and I hope they find value in the information I've assembled.

Ultimately, my goal in writing this book, however, is to save you—*the home buyer*—heartache and money. I want you to feel confident when you write an offer or agree to a counteroffer that you're making a good deal backed by solid information. I promise that if you put the information in this book to work, your home-buying experience will be an exciting, fulfilling life event—not a financial disaster or confusing nightmare. Whether you're a first-time buyer or you've bought and sold several homes, I know this book will show you ways to improve the home-buying experience, making it more successful and less stressful.

Join me now and become a savvy home buying shopper!

# CHAPTER 1
## ARE YOU READY TO BUY A HOME?

*I purchased my first home back in 1977 in Mission Viejo, CA. My first husband and I were in our mid-20s, and I remember very little about the process except that my mom loaned us the down payment, and we signed a whole stack of papers that I really didn't understand. I don't even think we negotiated the sales price, and I know we definitely didn't shop for a loan. We basically just followed what our agent told us to do. Luckily for us, our agent was trustworthy and the market was in an upswing. When we sold three years later, we more than doubled our money, but we could have just as easily lost it due to our ignorance.*

While buying a home is a lifelong dream for many, it's also a complicated process that comes with considerable responsibility. In this chapter, I'll be taking you through the pros and cons of homeownership to help you determine if buying a home is right for you at this point in your life. But before we dive in, let's look at a typical example:

*Ashley and Todd just made the last payment on their current 12-month lease for the condo they've been renting here in San Diego for the past two years.*

*Their landlord calls to let them know that when they renew the lease, the monthly payment will be going up by $200! They certainly didn't see that coming!*

*So now they're seriously considering buying a home, but they're getting all kinds of advice from friends and family that's only making the decision more confusing. Do they have enough money saved? What if one of them loses their job? What if they buy a lemon that becomes a money pit?*

There are many legitimate concerns about buying a home. It is the single largest purchase most people will make in their lifetime. And, obviously, there are some things that happen in life that can't be anticipated. To help take the guesswork out of it, I've put together some of the pros and cons of home-ownership and a list of 12 statements you'll want to consider before making the move.

## Pros

**Stability.** One of the biggest drawbacks to renting is the uncertainty of not knowing how long you will be able to stay in one location. When you rent, where you live and for how long is at the whim of your landlord or property manager. When you own your own single-family home or condo, so long as you pay your mortgage, it is unlikely that any outside party can force you to move.

**Predictable payments.** If you purchase a home with a fixed-rate mortgage, your monthly payment will not change, whereas monthly rents can change annually or even monthly, depending on your contract. Knowing that your housing expense is fixed makes it much easier to plan for other purchases, such as vacations and cars.

**Mortgage interest and property taxes paid are tax deductible.** These added deductions can represent a significant tax savings that you don't have if paying rent.

**Building equity.** With the economy back on more stable ground, we have seen significant appreciation in property values over the past few years. Although the pace has slowed a bit, home values are still increasing, which means that as values increase, and as you pay down your principal, you are creating equity that you can tap into for college, retirement, or for buying a step-up home in the future.

This is a strong argument for homeownership. Right now, the average rent in San Diego County for a decent two-bedroom condo is around $1650. That is $19,800 a year, and in just five years, that adds up to $99,000! Nearly $100,000 and nothing to show for it.

**Investment opportunity.** Depending on the price and monthly expenses, it might be that the first home you buy can later be rented out, allowing you to derive rental income. Now you're the landlord! Many first-time buyers often purchase a more modest first home with this strategy in mind.

**Putting down roots.** One of the less obvious benefits of homeownership is people often feel more connected to a community when they own a home in a specific area, and they're more likely to participate or volunteer in local activities or groups.

**Decorate as you desire.** Another drawback to renting is the lack of freedom to make your own decorating decisions when it comes to paint, wallpaper, or even updating faucets and light fixtures. When you own your home, you can let the DIY decorator in you run free!

## Cons

**It takes money. Lots of money.** While there are some loan programs (VA and some credit unions) that require zero down, generally you need at least 3.5% of the purchase price as a down payment for an FHA loan. Conventional loans require 5–20%. That is a lot of money for many people to save.

There are some down payment assistance programs available, and often a seller will help with closing costs. Alternately, buyers often borrow from their retirement accounts or get gift funds from a family member. If you decide to buy, obtaining a pre-approval for a loan will be your first step before looking at homes! Knowing what you can honestly afford will save you disappointment down the road. I'll have more on the pre-approval process in Chapter 3.

**You might have to give up some things.** Let's say you want to buy a home for $425,000 with an FHA loan. You put down $14,875. With your upfront mortgage insurance premium written into the loan, your loan amount is $417,302. Your monthly payment—including principal, interest, mortgage insurance, taxes, and homeowner's insurance—will be roughly $2,946.00. Depending on where you are purchasing, a single-family home priced at $425,000 might not have a remodeled kitchen or bathrooms, and it is likely you will have to make some cuts in other expenditures, such as entertainment, in order to afford the home.

**If it breaks, you fix it.** The nice part about renting is that if the water heater bursts, not only is the owner responsible for replacing or repairing it, but they also have to clean up any mess or damage. You own it, you fix it. This can come as quite a shock to new homeowners, and it is recommended that you have some funds in reserve to cope with unexpected repairs or appliances that need to be replaced. The amount of reserves will vary, but lenders often recommend that home-owners have six months PITI (Principal, Interest, Taxes, and Insurance) saved to cover unexpected repairs or loss of income. Not everything is covered by insurance or home warranties.

**Ongoing maintenance.** Owning a home or condo has varying levels of maintenance that must be taken care of in order to protect your investment. If you have a single-family home with a yard, you will have regular maintenance, or you'll need to hire a gardener. There will also be numerous other ongoing projects, like cleaning the rain gutters or pest control. On the other hand, if you purchase a condo, expect to pay an average of $280-$400 a month in homeowners' association (HOA) fees to cover maintenance for the complex.

## What to Consider

Here are some statements to consider that will help you determine if you are ready to be a homeowner, and if so, whether you would be more comfortable in a condo or single-family home.

1. I like where I live and haven't given much thought to buying.

2. I really enjoy having a swimming pool and gym where I live.

3. I have a steady job and have managed to save some money.

4. I hate the idea of paying rent and having nothing to show for it.

5. I like the idea of moving from city to city to see more of the country.

6. I pay a lot in taxes and would like to have some additional deductions.

7. I consider myself handy and enjoy getting my hands dirty.

8. I don't spend much time at home on evenings or weekends.

9. I'd like to have a place for my kids and/or dog to play outdoors.

10. I honestly don't get bored watching HGTV or DIY Channel.

11. I'm okay with cutting back on dinners out and entertainment to pay a mortgage.

12. I like knowing that I don't have to move unless I want to.

SAVVY SHOPPER TIPS: Don't buy unless you're ready, and make sure you purchase the type of property best suited for who you are and how you like to live—it's a big commitment.

If you're tired of moving and looking for some stability, and if you have a steady, reliable income, you might be ready to buy—at least psychologically. If you're handy, enjoy DIY projects, and want some outdoor space, a single-family home might be your best buy. On the other hand, if you like amenities, such as a pool and fitness room, and are not interested in the responsibility of ongoing maintenance, a condo would probably be more suitable. If you don't mind moving every couple of years and would rather spend your money on travel and/or entertainment or cars, you're probably not a good candidate for buying at this time.

Ready to buy? Let's take the next step!

# CHAPTER 2
## GETTING YOUR DUCKS IN A ROW

W hether you're shopping for your first home or your third, contrary to what you might see on TV, the home buying process does not begin with your real estate agent showing you a home you can't afford. It actually should begin as much as a year in advance with a careful evaluation of your credit.

> *My friends Ashley and Todd, who we met in Chapter 1, made the decision that they were ready to buy. So they went to the bank where they both had accounts and started the application process. The loan officer ran both of their credit reports but discovered a problem. Apparently, several years earlier while still in college, Todd had run up some serious credit card debt and defaulted on two cards that were now showing as collection accounts, along with three delinquent parking tickets. Todd had managed to maintain another credit card and a car loan, so he hadn't really thought about these black marks as being significant until now. The loan officer explained that these derogatory items would have to be removed before Todd could be on the loan. Disappointed, they realized they would probably have to continue to rent until Todd's credit issues were resolved.*

In order to purchase a home, most people need a home loan. There are several different types of loans offered by banks, credit unions, and mortgage bankers. The type of loan you can get and the interest rate you will be charged is largely determined by your credit score, which is affected by a number of factors, including your payment history, the length of time you've had credit, derogatory items, and the level of debt you carry in relation to credit limits.

When evaluating your credit for a mortgage pre-approval, a lender will pull what is called a tri-merge report. This is one report that shows your credit history and score according to the three primary credit bureaus: Experian, Equifax, and TransUnion. *The lender will use the middle score, not the highest, among the three reports. And if there are two buyers, they will use the middle score of the lower-scoring buyer.* This is why it's important to check your credit reports from all three bureaus, not just one.

Most people will discover some discrepancies on their reports, or items that are simply erroneous. Some of these items you can correct fairly easily by writing the bureau in question and providing written proof of your claim. But there are other issues that may be more challenging, such as accounts listed in your name that you've never had, or collection accounts or late payments that were actually paid on time. In some situations, it may be helpful to consult with a reputable credit repair agency to see what you can fix, what you may need to just wait out, or what they can do to help. The credit repair process can take as much as a year, but it will be well worth it if you are able to improve your score and get a more favorable rate for your mortgage.

One note of caution about debt settlement programs. If you have a lot of unsecured debt (credit cards), it may be tempting to employ the services of a debt settlement company thinking this will be a good way to restore your credit. Basically, you stop paying your creditors and you make one payment a month to the debt settlement company. They then negotiate a settlement payment with each of your creditors. These programs generally take 18–48 months to complete, and in the meantime, your credit is ruined because you've stopped making payments to your creditors. If your debt is substantial and you see no way out, it might be wise to consult a bankruptcy attorney and put home buying on the back burner.

However, one relatively quick fix to boost your score if you don't have a lot of derogatory items is to pay down the balance on your credit cards to less than 30% of your credit limit. What you don't want to do, however, is close accounts, especially old ones. Better to keep it open with a zero balance, or just use it and pay it off occasionally. This helps maintain a favorable ratio of total debt to available credit. If you close accounts, your ratio becomes less favorable.

So, how high of a score do you need to qualify for a home loan? Lenders make interest rate determinations based on tiered rate sheets: As scores go down, rates go up. 580 is generally considered on the low end for an FHA loan, and 620 is the minimum for conventional financing. 760 is considered a great score with very low risk to lenders, so with scores upwards of 760, interest rates don't really get that much better. There are loans available for very low scores, but these are generally termed "hard money" loans and require at least a 30% down payment. They also charge at least 2 points (1 point = 1% of your loan amount), and they carry very high interest rates. It should be noted, though, that every lender has slightly different guidelines and rate sheets, which is why it pays to shop for your loan, as you may get a better deal with one lender over another. More on this in Chapter 3.

## Disputing Items on Your Credit Reports

All three major credit report bureaus have systems for consumers to dispute items on their credit reports, and that includes specific forms they ask you to complete. Please note they will not review your disputed items over the phone, so don't waste your time. The best way to make sure you have the most up-to-date information regarding the dispute procedures for each bureau is to Google them. For instance, use the keywords "Experian disputes" or "TransUnion disputes." Then make sure the link is pointing you to the website of the actual credit bureau in question. Each bureau will outline for you exactly what form to submit and how the procedure works.

Before you contact them, make sure you have a current report from each bureau, as they will request the file number of the report. If you see something you think is inaccurate, such as a late car payment, it would be a good idea to first try to resolve the issue with the creditor by contacting them to dispute the payment date. This could be done by providing bank statements or online payment confirmation numbers.

Here are the addresses for sending dispute forms:

Experian
P.O. Box 4500
Allen, TX 75013

Experian also has an online form you can fill out: *https://experian.com/consumer/upload/*

*TransUnion Consumer Solutions*
P.O. Box 2000
Chester, PA 19022–2000

*Equifax Information Services, LLC*
P.O. Box 740256
Atlanta, GA 30374

> SAVVY SHOPPER TIPS: Check your credit reports from all three major credit reporting bureaus 9 to 12 months prior to when you want to start looking for a home. If you find inaccuracies, take the time to contact each bureau and dispute the information. If you are unsure about how to proceed to remove certain items, consult with a reputable credit repair organization and retain their services if needed to clean up derogatory items. It is worth spending some money now to improve your score, as it will allow you to save money for years with a lower interest rate on your mortgage.

# CHAPTER 3
## LOAN PRE-APPROVAL
## TIME TO GET REAL

The next step in the home-buying process has nothing to do with searching online for the home of your dreams. It actually begins with a reality check as you go through the pre-approval process and learn exactly how much you can really afford. There is absolutely no value in looking at homes that are outside your price range, as it's just a waste of everyone's time and a source of disappointment and discouragement.

*About a year ago, the adult child of one of my dear friends gave me a call and said that he was ready to start looking for a condo to purchase. I was so excited for him to be taking this big step! We talked about what he could afford, and he mentioned that he'd already been to his credit union. They had run the numbers and pre-qualified him for a zero-down-payment loan of up to $325,000. He had a credit score close to 800, so the loan officer said everything should be fine. We were both excited and started our search. After just a couple of weeks, I found a wonderful condo that was close to his work and in a very desirable area—it really felt more like a single-family home. We wrote an offer and with very little back and forth,*

*our offer was accepted! We were so excited. Every-*
*thing was submitted to the lender and my buyer con-*
*tinued by signing property disclosures and even pay-*
*ing for a full property inspection.*

*Then, everything unexpectedly fell apart. Even*
*though my buyer was currently making more than*
*enough to qualify with his current debt-to-income ra-*
*tio, he worked on commission and did not have*
*enough time showing that he could maintain that*
*level of income. They looked only at his last two years'*
*income tax returns, and based on that, he did not*
*make enough to qualify. We were both crushed!*

## Pre-Qualification vs. Pre-Approval

First, it's important to know the difference between pre-qualification and pre-approval. A *pre-qualification* is usually done
by a mortgage broker or lender, either in person or over the
phone. You provide information regarding your income,
debts, assets, and potential down payment. The lender will
then probably run your credit. Feeding this information into
specialized software, the lender will provide you with a ball-
park figure for the size and type of loan for which you would
likely qualify. There is no commitment, but a pre-qualification will at least give you an idea of the price range you can
afford and the types of programs and interest rates offered by
that lender. **In the case of my friend noted above, the loan**
**officer seemed to think that his high score would do the**
**trick, but she had neglected to ask him how long he had**
**been making commission at his current level.**

A *pre-approval*, on the other hand, carries more weight,
as all of your information is verified and often run through
Desktop Underwriting (DU) software, which provides a

written approval, subject to certain conditions, including the appraisal and title report. Although every lender is slightly different, here are the basic items you will need to provide to get pre-approval:

- Signed authorization form supplied by your lender to run your credit report.

- A signed loan application created by your lender.

- 2–3 months' pay statements.

- W-2s for the last two years.

- *Signed* federal tax returns for the last two years.

- Bank and/or retirement account statements (all accounts, all pages, even if blank) for the last 2–3 months.

- Letters of explanation for any derogatory items that appear on your credit report.

- If you are self-employed, you may need to supply 1099s and profit and loss statements.

## *Working with a Lender*

When submitting your documents to the lender, it is best to scan the items as separate PDF files or send them as separate faxes. Submitting original bank statements and tax returns will slow down your approval process, as a loan processor will have to scan and organize everything into files that can be uploaded to the underwriters.

Another thing to keep in mind is that you are not committed to working with a lender simply because they did a pre-approval for you. By the time you have submitted all of your information, it may be much simpler to stay with them, but you should always shop at least one other lender to see who can provide the best rate and terms. Often times, if you get a better quote, you can go back to your original lender and see if they can match it.

You may want to consider your bank or credit union, as they often offer a small interest rate discount if you elect automatic payment for your mortgage from your existing bank account. On the other hand, a mortgage broker represents a number of different lenders and may have a wider variety of loan products from which to choose.

And, of course, there are many online options, such as LendingTree or Quicken Loans. What you might not understand, however, is that these companies are basically lead generators for mortgage brokers. This means that when you complete an online application, your information is sold and instantly delivered to several different companies. You will be immediately contacted by phone and email... over and over again. This is not all bad, as they truly are competing for your business. But if you are going to go this route, just pick two companies and let them bring out their best quotes.

One concern about shopping for a loan is that it will harm your credit score to have your credit run several times. The good news is that if your credit is run within a short period of time, say three times in one month by three different lenders, it is unlikely that there will be any negative impact on your score, as it is obvious that you are shopping for a loan. However, multiple inquiries *are* a problem when you're applying for several different store credit cards or a variety of credit types in a short period of time, such as a car loan, a Visa or MasterCard, *and* a mortgage. Avoid applying for any other type of credit during the home purchase process; this includes applying for credit to buy appliances right before closing. The added inquiries and debt could be enough to disqualify you from your home loan!

By the time you get to the pre-approval stage, you should have been working on improving your credit score, as described in Chapter 2, and you should be ready to go. Your pre-approval letter is an important tool used by your real estate agent as part of any offer to purchase, as it provides proof that you are qualified to complete the transaction. It will include information about the type of loan, the loan size, and the price point at which you can purchase. It will also include information about the other conditions that must be met for final approval, such as clear title and sufficient appraised value.

Generally, it is a good idea to know your maximum loan amount, but you'll want to have a pre-approval letter written specific to the amount you are offering. For instance, if you are qualified for a $400,000 loan with a 20% down payment, that would mean you could purchase a home for $500,000. But let's say you find a great home and want to offer $425,000. That would mean your loan amount would be $340,000. From a negotiating point of view, it may be better to submit a pre-approval letter for a $425,000 purchase price with a $340,000 loan amount and not reveal how much more you could actually spend. There is no need for the seller to know that you could actually afford another $75,000! Talk to your loan officer about this and make sure they are willing to provide customized approval letters based on the price you are offering.

First-time buyers frequently ask if they can get a loan for more than the amount needed to purchase the home and use the excess funds for upgrades, remodeling, or new appliances. Generally speaking, the answer is "no." The house is collateral for the lender, and in case of default, the bank wants to make sure it can sell the home and recoup its funds without a loss. That is why an appraisal is so important. The bank needs assurance that the sales price is not artificially inflated, such as what we saw before the housing crash. The exception to this is a rehab loan, where the bank is actually lending on the value of the home as it is estimated to be after repairs. This is a more complicated loan process and not recommended for first-time buyers.

SAVVY SHOPPER TIPS: Shop around to at least two lenders to see who will give you the best rate and terms. Submit all of your documentation to your selected lender, and ask for a full pre-approval—not just a pre-qualification—so you know the maximum loan amount for which you qualify to avoid any surprises or disappointments. When submitting documents, don't send a bunch of originals unless it can't be avoided. Don't apply for other types of credit during the home purchase process. When writing an offer, submit a pre-approval letter with the approved loan amount being specific to your offered price.

# CHAPTER 4
## FINDING THE LOAN
## THAT'S RIGHT FOR YOU

*Back in 2006, at the height of the housing market, I was working as a loan officer. As we know, it was a crazy time in the world of lending, when even the most conservative banks would underwrite a loan for basically anyone with a pulse. People were using their homes like ATM machines. As home values continued to climb, some owners were refinancing and draining their equity as fast as it accumulated.*

*One of the craziest loans popular at that time was the negative amortization loan (NegAm). This loan allowed the borrower to make a minimum payment each month that was less than an interest-only payment. The amount of the unpaid interest was added to the principal amount owed so that each month, instead of paying down the loan, the debt actually increased up to a certain threshold above the original loan amount. With the availability of a loan that allowed one to make a minimum payment at a starter rate as low as 1%, it was very tempting to buy a home that was more expensive than one could really afford.*

*When the housing bubble burst, the people with NegAm loans got a one-two punch. Not only had home values dropped by as much as 50%, but they had increased the amount they owed by tens of thousands of dollars. The people who successfully rode out the storm and managed to keep their homes were the ones who did not drain all of their equity, and if they did refinance, had selected a traditional loan.*

Although safeguards are now in place to help prevent the kind of disaster we saw in the housing crash, selecting the loan that is right for you is still one of the biggest decisions you'll make when buying a home. In this chapter, I take you through the various loan products and their key characteristics to help you in the decision-making process.

## Government-Insured and Conventional Loans

Government-insured loans are backed by the U.S. Government, meaning that the government insures the lender against loss in case of default. Government-insured loans include FHA, VA, and USDA. Conventional loans, on the other hand, are not insured by the government.

## FHA Loans

The primary advantage of an FHA loan is that the buyer can have a down payment as low as 3.5% of the purchase price, which makes home buying more accessible to a larger number of people. The disadvantage is that you will pay an upfront monthly mortgage insurance premium (MIP) until you have paid down the amount you owe and have 20% equity in the home. At that point, you will probably have to request that your lender remove the MIP, as this is not something that automatically happens. This insurance premium is added to your monthly mortgage payment, increasing your overall monthly payment.

## VA Loans

VA loans are available only to military service members and their families. They offer a huge benefit in that no down payment is required. You will be required to pay a funding fee of 1.25–3.30%, but that is generally written into the loan amount.

## USDA Loans

USDA loans are offered by the U.S. Department of Agriculture to encourage homeownership in rural areas. These loans also have low down-payment requirements, but they're only available in specific areas, and buyers must meet income requirements. USDA loans can be a good choice if you're in a designated rural area and have a modest income.

## Conventional Loans

Conventional loans are simply loans that are not insured by the government. Generally speaking, they require a minimum 5% down payment, and you will likely be required to pay private mortgage insurance (PMI) if your down payment is less than 20%. As noted in the discussion about FHA loans, the mortgage insurance is paid until there is 20% equity in the property.

## Conforming and Non-Conforming (Jumbo) Loans

The terms "conforming" and "non-conforming" (or jumbo) relate primarily to the maximum size of the loan amount.

*Conforming loans* meet the underwriting guidelines of Fannie Mae and Freddie Mac, which are government-controlled corporations. Fannie and Freddie basically buy loans and re-sell them in the secondary market on Wall Street. In order to sell these mortgage-backed securities and reduce the risk to buyers, they have established specific underwriting criteria, including limiting the size of a loan. The baseline maximum conforming loan limit for most counties across the US is $453,100. For areas with higher housing costs, such as New York, San Francisco, San Diego, and Washington, DC, the limit is higher.

*Non-conforming* or *jumbo loans* exceed the maximum loan amounts of conforming loans and do not necessarily adhere to the Fannie and Freddie underwriting guidelines. As these loans represent a great risk to the lender and the ultimate buyer of the loan, they are offered at a higher interest rate.

## Fixed- and Adjustable-Rate Mortgages

*Fixed-rate mortgages* have the same interest rate and monthly payment over the entire length of the loan. They are fully amortizing, so at the end of the loan term, the principal amount and all interest charges are paid in full. A fixed-rate loan is good in the sense that there are no surprises or changes. However, in a period where interest rates are declining, a borrower would have to bear the cost of refinancing in order to take advantage of the declining rates. The rates are also slightly higher than adjustable-rate mortgages, as you are in essence buying the stability of no rate changes.

*Adjustable-rate mortgages* (*ARM*) have interest rates that will adjust at certain periods. Generally, there is an initial fixed rate for two or five years, after which the interest rate will adjust every year according to a particular monetary index. For example, a 5/1 ARM is fixed for the first five years and then adjusts every year thereafter. The biggest advantage to an ARM is the initial fixed rate is always lower than a 30-year fixed-rate mortgage. This is especially attractive to buyers who anticipate an increase in income over the coming years, as this lower starting rate allows them to afford a more expensive house than they might otherwise be able to buy. This is also a smart choice for buyers who know that they will live in the home for a limited time period. The disadvantage of ARMs is that they're confusing, and many borrowers have been caught off-guard when their loan adjusts, simply not being ready for an increase in payments. On the other hand, if rates decline, they will automatically benefit without the expense of refinancing.

## Buying with a Reverse Mortgage

Most people, many real estate professionals included, are unaware that a person 62 years of age or older can utilize a reverse mortgage known as the *Home Equity Conversion Mortgage (HECM)* for the purchase of a property. Passed by Congress in 2009, a senior can use a non-recourse FHA reverse mortgage to buy a home and never pay another mortgage payment unless they want to.

Here's an example of how this works: A 72-year-old homeowner wants to downsize and sells his home for $650,000, clearing $300,000 after commissions and expenses. He then finds a better-suited home for $550,000 and puts down $250,000. The reverse mortgage makes up the $300,000 difference, and the homeowner keeps the remaining $50,000 to spend as he chooses, and he never needs to make another mortgage payment.

The older the homebuyer, the less a down payment is required. Over time, the loan balance increases, and at the time the homeowner dies, the heirs have the option of paying off the balance of the reverse mortgage and keeping the home, or selling the home and pocketing the equity. Should the value of the home be less than the loan balance, the heirs can refinance or sell the home to pay off the loan at 95% of fair market value, not loan balance—FHA covers the deficiency, and there is no deficiency judgment against the heirs.

One important advantage of the program is that qualifying is much easier than for a traditional loan. Seniors often have very limited income, so a reverse mortgage is perfect, as there are no FICO guidelines and very limited income requirements. According to the US Census Bureau, of the 21.6 million homes owned by persons aged 65 or older, 65%—or 14.1 million homes—are owned free and clear. Thus, many seniors are house-rich but cash poor.

## Loan Terms—How Long Will You Pay?

A basic rule of thumb is the longer the term of your loan, the lower your monthly payment, but the more interest you'll pay over the life of the loan. So, for instance, a $300,000 loan at a fixed rate of 3.75% for 30 years is $1,389.00 a month, principle and interest. The total interest paid over 30 years is $200,165. To pay off that same loan in 15 years, the monthly principle and interest payment would be $2,181, and the total interest paid would be just $92,700—less than half as much.

For most first-time buyers, a longer term may be advantageous, as the monthly payments will be lower. This is also true for people who plan on a future move, where paying down the principle might not make much sense. On the other hand, if you have found your forever home, it might be a good idea to pay off your home early while you're still working and then own it free and clear in retirement. Another scenario where it might make sense to accelerate your payments would be to gain 20% equity so you can eliminate PMI from your monthly loan.

If you're interested in a shorter loan length, instead of applying for a 15-year mortgage, you might consider getting a 30-year mortgage and then making your payments based on a 15-year payoff, which is a calculation you can easily make online. In this way, if you have a month or two where you are unable to make the higher payment, you're not in a position of possibly missing a payment or defaulting. Your interest rate might be slightly higher, but you have greater flexibility in determining your payments.

Please keep in mind these different types of mortgages work in combination with one another. For example, you could get a fixed-rate FHA loan or an adjustable-rate VA loan, or vice-versa; a fixed-rate conforming conventional loan or an adjustable-rate non-conforming jumbo loan. The real key to finding the right loan lies in finding a qualified loan officer who can help explain in detail the pros and cons of each loan type and help you select the mortgage best suited to your specific needs and long-term plans.

SAVVY SHOPPER TIPS: Make sure you discuss your plans for this home purchase with your loan officer, including the estimated time you plan to live in the home. It is also important to be very clear with your loan officer about the source of your down payment and exactly how much money you have available. If you are considering an ARM loan, make sure you thoroughly understand when your rate will adjust, how the adjustment is calculated, and approximately what you might be looking at in terms of a payment increase. Although we no longer see pre-payment penalties very often, do confirm that there is no penalty for paying off your loan before it is due. And finally, if you are 62 or older, I strongly suggest that you explore the HECM Reverse Mortgage for Seniors program.

# CHAPTER 5
## THE COST OF BUYING
## WHERE TO FIND DOWN PAYMENT HELP

F or many people, especially first-time home buyers, one of the toughest things to do is save money for a down payment. Even with an FHA loan, a 3.5% down payment can be a lot of money. To purchase a $450,000 home with an FHA loan in San Diego County, you would need $15,750, plus money to cover closing costs. (We'll talk more about closing costs in Chapter 11.) That is a tall order, especially when living in an area with expensive rents and an overall high cost of living.

## *Down Payment Assistance Programs*

What most buyers don't know is that there are over 2,000 different down payment assistance programs throughout the US, and at least one program is available in each of the country's 3,142 counties. What's more, over 2,000 counties have at least 10 programs available. One common misconception is that these programs are only available to first-time buyers when, in fact, qualification is primarily based on income level (which will vary according to the market and the needs of a specific area). For instance, the Department of Housing and Urban Development (HUD) provides states with block grants to fund the Neighborhood Stabilization Program, which is designed to revitalize the areas hardest hit with fore-closures and unemployment during the recession.

Down payment assistance programs basically fall into two categories: grants and second mortgages. Grants are funds that do not have to be repaid, provided you live in the home for a certain period of time. The second mortgages have very low or even zero-interest rates, and the payments are deferred over a certain period of time—or in some cases, the loan is cancelled. Many of these programs also allow the funds to be used in part to cover closing costs.

The best resource I've found for researching available pro-grams is Down Payment Resource, an online aggregator of down payment assistance programs throughout the country. You can visit them here: *http://downpaymentresource.com.*

## Gift Money

Another form of assistance is gifted money. Most lenders will allow gift money from a family member if the donor signs an approved gift letter stating that the funds are indeed a gift that does not have to be repaid. Family loans are generally not allowed, as the debt could become an additional lien on the property and would count against your debt-to-income ratio. The percentage of the down payment that can be a gift varies according to the type of loan, and the actual amount given may have tax implications for the donor. Currently, the IRS does not impose a gift tax on amounts of $14,000 or less, and a married couple who files jointly can gift up to $28,000 with-out being taxed.[1] So, if your uncle wants to give you $5,000 to help you buy your first home, that should be fine. Just make

---

1. US Tax Center, "7 Things You Should Know About Gift Tax," US Tax Center, October 07, 2014, accessed June 2018, https://www.irs.com/ar-ticles/7-things-you-should-know-about-gift-tax.

sure you discuss with your lender about any necessary paper-work, as well as when and how the funds should be trans-ferred.

Before we wrap up this section on gift money, I'd like to share a story with you.

*Several years ago, I had the pleasure of working with a young couple buying their first home in San Diego. They both had good jobs, but really didn't have quite enough for the FHA down payment. The wife con-tacted her mother who lived in a small Eastern Euro-pean village to ask for assistance. Her mom, who was quite old, said she would be happy to gift her daugh-ter and son-in-law $8,000.*

*The problem we ran into was unexpected. At this point in time, her mom still used a passbook for the bank to manually record all of her deposits and with-drawals from her savings account. That passbook was her only record, as she received no monthly state-ments. The lender, in order to comply with anti-ter-rorist laws that require all funds to be sourced, was demanding a bank statement showing the funds le-gitimately belonged to her mom, but all she had was her passbook.*

*The whole deal nearly fell apart. The buyer's mom was confused, and even though the bank made a pho-tocopy of her passbook and managed to fax it to me, the lender was not satisfied as to the source of the money. Given the time difference for phone calls, and the age of her mother, my buyer was very concerned that this whole transaction was becoming too difficult for her mother. She was so upset that she ended up in tears, wanting to cancel the purchase.*

*Finally, I got through to a senior manager at the lender, and he was able to sign-off on the funds transfer, satisfied that this elderly woman was not a terrorist trying to launder money! What I learned from this is to always make sure gift funds are in order before writing an offer!*

## Seller Assistance

Another source of funds might be the sellers, depending on the amount of equity they have in the home and their plans after selling. If a seller owns a property outright, or has a large amount of equity, they might consider taking back a second mortgage at a reasonable interest rate. Again, this would be important to discuss with your lender, prior to writing an offer requesting any type of seller financing. You might also want to consider asking the seller to cover a certain amount of your closing costs. In some cases, it might make sense to pay a slightly higher price for the home if the seller covers some of your costs. From the seller's perspective, they might be willing to cover some of your costs if the price is high enough to net the same amount as a lower price with no closing costs.

## Borrowing from Your Retirement Account

There are definitely pros and cons to borrowing from your 401K account or liquidating your IRA, depending on the type of account you have. There may be age-related penalties and/or tax consequences. In any case, your lender will require documentation showing all terms and whether or not you plan to repay, or if you're liquidating funds from the account.

It you are borrowing from your retirement account, please remember that this new loan will be calculated into your debt-to-income ratio, meaning that you will be able to afford less on a monthly basis in terms of a mortgage payment.

SAVVY SHOPPER TIPS: Explore your down payment options with your loan officer and real estate agent as part of your pre-approval process. That way, you know the source of your funds before you set out on your home search. If looking for a down payment assistance program, keep in mind that the application process might take more than 30 days. If using gifted funds from a family member, make sure to confirm with your lender the exact gift letter form that must be used and when and how funds should be transferred. If trying to secure funds from the seller, ask your real estate agent to research the balance on what the seller still owes on the home to see if a seller contribution is even feasible. Keep in mind that in order for your offer to be competitive, you may need to offer a higher price to off-set any seller contribution. If looking to use your retirement account, always walk through the numbers with your accountant to see if this is a wise move.

# CHAPTER 6
## YOUR SECRET WEAPON
## A KILLER AGENT

In an age when there seems to be an app for everything, including finding homes, some might say that the role of the real estate agent is becoming obsolete. After all, with public access to local MLS searches and home value websites, who needs an agent to help them buy a home?

You do. Buying a home is not like buying a pair of shoes, or even a car. This is a huge investment that you will be paying off for years. *The home purchase transaction is rather like an iceberg; what you see above water may seem manageable, but it's what lies below the surface that can send a deal crashing.* Here are just a few of the services a qualified buyer's agent will provide you:

- Send you online listings of all the homes that fit your parameters.

- Keep you updated when new homes come on the market.

- Research market value so that you don't overpay.

- Write a compelling offer.

- Negotiate the sales price and terms on your behalf.

- Suggest questions to ask about a property, such as permits or zoning.

- Negotiate for repairs on your behalf.

- Provide referrals for trusted inspectors, painters, and other contractors.

- Make sure that all disclosures and other legal paperwork are completed properly.

- You pay nothing! The seller pays the buyer's agent at closing. You benefit from all of their expertise at no cost to you!

## Finding an Agent

So, how do you select the best real estate agent to assist you in your home-buying quest? Here are a few tips and questions to ask before making a final decision:

- *Ask your friends for referrals.* Who have they worked with who they felt did a great job for them?

- *Do not call the listing agent on a property that you'd like to view and ask them to represent you.* Their primary obligation is to the seller, so their ability to negotiate on your behalf may be conflicted. (More on dual agency later in this chapter.)

- *Whether you find a real estate agent online or through a personal referral, be sure to Google any prospective real estate agent.* There should be several results, with perhaps a website and blog, as well as profiles on sites like Realtor.com, Zillow, Trulia, Facebook, LinkedIn, and

Yelp. In an age when internet marketing is key, you need an agent who is at least fairly tech savvy.

- *Meet with them in person as soon as possible, at their office or a coffee shop, before viewing homes.* This is a professional relationship, but you want to make sure you feel comfortable with one another, as trust and compatibility are important. This will also give you an opportunity to measure the agent's professionalism, as well as their openness to really listen to your needs and desires. If all they do is talk about their personal success, this is probably not the agent you want.

- *If you know the part of town where you hope to purchase, make sure your agent is familiar with the area.* You want to be sure they can offer constructive information about the various neighborhoods.

- *Ask them if they are a full-time agent.* This is a very competitive market, and you want to be working with an agent who is on top of the latest listings and getting you into those new properties as quickly as possible. Hot properties are often gone within hours, so working with someone who is only working part-time definitely puts you at a disadvantage.

- *Ask how long they have been licensed.* As with most professions, experience is important. That being said, there are many good agents who are relatively new in the business. If their experience seems minimal, ask them about the type of brokerage support that's available in case you have questions they can't answer or a problem arises.

- *What is their protocol for responding to your calls, emails, or texts?* What is their average response time? Will you be working with them directly throughout the process, or will they be sending someone else to show you properties? Nothing is worse than being in the middle of your house hunt or transaction and feeling like your agent has abandoned you.

- *Ask any prospective agent for testimonials from past clients.* You should also check for reviews on Yelp, Trulia, Zillow, and Google. However, while some real estate agents are very good about remembering to ask clients to leave feedback, a real estate agent isn't necessarily less qualified just because they have few reviews.

- *Are they a REALTOR?* In California, licensees are either salespersons or brokers, often referred to as agents. REALTOR is a designation used by salespersons and brokers who are also members of the National, State, and Local Association of REALTORS. It is not mandatory to join the associations, but members do subscribe to a code of ethics and may spend more time on their professional education.

- *Check their license status.* In California, you can look up any licensee at the Department of Real Estate (*www.dre.ca.gov*). Here you can check to make sure their license is current and whether it has ever been suspended or revoked. You can also see if there has ever been any disciplinary action or fines. Other states have similar online services.

Finding the right agent is an important step, as this person will be your guide throughout the home-buying process. Not only should they be well-versed in real estate, but they should also care about your needs. That being said, I'd like to share a personal story:

> *As I mentioned in Chapter 1, I bought my first home when I was 25, and I had no clue about how to select a real estate agent. My husband and I were renting a nice home in Mission Viejo, and one of our neighbors was a real estate agent. He spoke to us about the possibility of buying, which really got us thinking. However, we didn't end up hiring him (which I'm sure seemed very odd to him). He was just a bit too flashy in his brand new Cadillac and seemed more interested in talking about himself than really understanding our needs. We were barely ex-Hippies, so we ended up with an agent who was a bit more low key—and his Cadillac was older. :) I have no recollection as to how we found him, but I'm just thankful that he turned out to be reasonably competent since we had no idea what we were doing!*

## Buyer Representation Agreements

Most buyers' agents will ask you to sign a representation agreement, which might make some buyers nervous. However, this actually protects you by providing contractual assurance that your agent will work diligently on your behalf. Remember, real estate agents are generally not paid until escrow closes, so all of the work they do researching and showing homes earns them no money.

When a real estate agent knows that a buyer is committed to working with them, they are much more likely to expend 100% effort. On the other hand, if the agent knows that the buyer is working with one or more other agents (thus lowering their odds of ever being paid), they're far less motivated to go all in. It's also much more convenient (and less confusing) for you, the buyer, to be receiving calls, emails, and information from just one agent. If you are still a bit unsure about committing, sign for just three months. If you are actively house hunting, you should have either found a home to purchase in that time, or at least know one way or the other if this agent is the one for you.

## Dual Agency

What if you find the perfect house, but you haven't yet found a real estate agent to represent you? You're anxious to write an offer. Should you contact the listing agent to write one for you?

The answer to that is generally "no." This is probably not a good idea, and in several states it's actually illegal. On the one hand, in a competitive market, the seller's agent will know exactly what it will take for you to get your offer accepted, perhaps outbidding other offers. But will you overpay? Does the listing agent really have your best interests at heart? Or is the seller their first priority? And it's not just the offer and sales price that are at stake. Who will negotiate for you if there are repairs or other items that must be addressed?

A situation where the real estate agent represents both the seller and the buyer is referred to as *dual agency*; meaning, the real estate agent has an equal fiduciary responsibility to both the buyer and seller. In practice, however, the potential for conflict of interest is high, and as a buyer, it is unlikely that an agent trying to get the highest possible price for their seller will push very hard for the price and terms that represent *your* best deal.

Every state has laws of agency that govern the obligations of a salesperson to his or her client, be they a buyer or seller. While dual agency is currently legal in California, it is illegal in several states, and more states are hoping to make it illegal because of the potential conflict of interest.

So what do you do? You've found your dream home, but you don't have an agent! One option is to ask the listing agent for a referral to another agent in their brokerage, or even in another brokerage, to represent you. Be clear with the listing agent that while you're sure they're a great agent, you are simply not comfortable with a dual-agency situation. While each situation must be evaluated on its own merit, being a buyer in a dual-agency situation is probably not in your best interest.

---

SAVVY SHOPPER TIPS: Do your online research, and then meet your prospective real estate agent in person. Interview more than one if you have any question about whether the first agent is the right one for you. Don't be afraid to ask questions. Remember, you are interviewing them for a very important job! And finally, no matter how much you love a home, asking the listing agent to represent you may not be in your best interest.

---

# CHAPTER 7
## LET THE HOUSE-HUNTING FUN BEGIN!

*Several years ago, I was working with a lovely young couple looking to buy their first home. They said the main thing they were looking for was a single-family home close to their church, and otherwise they were pretty open. Luckily, at that time, there were quite a few homes available that fit their budget in their neighborhood of choice, so I was certain we would quickly be in escrow. What I soon discovered, however, was that they were completely unable to make a decision, and by the time they were ready to make an offer on a property, someone else had already beaten them to it.*

*This happened several times. It appeared that their "must-have" list was a moving target. One house was great except the back yard was a bit too small. Another didn't have a fireplace, and yet another had an extra room they didn't feel they needed. I don't think they had really discussed exactly what they were looking for besides the location and number of bedrooms. They were confused and unable to make a decision. They were convinced that something even better would come on the market tomorrow. After a very frustrating eight weeks, I suggested that maybe they needed to take a time-out and collect their thoughts about what they really wanted. They agreed.*

*We stayed in touch, but six months later, they moved out of state where they thought it would be easier to find their perfect home!*

*The first step* in your home search starts with understanding what you're looking for, and communicating that to your real estate agent. The more your real estate agent knows about your wants, needs, and qualifications, the quicker they will find you the right property. In the next section, I've put together some questions to get you thinking. Share the key points and "must-haves" with your real estate agent, and get ready to house hunt!

## The First Step: Buyer Questionnaire

1. Why do you want to buy a home? Have you previously purchased property, or is this your first experience?

2. Are you looking for a single-family home, or a condo? Will this be your primary residence, a second home, or a rental property?

3. How soon do you hope to complete the purchase? Are there any deadlines? Do you have a home to sell before you can buy?

4. Will you be paying cash or financing the purchase? If obtaining a mortgage, have you been pre-approved? What is your price range based on your pre-approval and available funds? Can you supply your real estate

agent with a copy of the pre-approval and proof of funds for the down payment and closing costs?

5. Is there a particular area or neighborhood that you would like to target? Are you willing to look outside your target area?

6. Is there a particular style of home you would love to have, or a style you would never consider?

7. How many bedrooms would be ideal? How many bathrooms? Do you want a formal dining area? Are there any other must-have rooms or features, such as an office, playroom, or man cave? What about a fireplace, A/C, RV parking, a walk-out basement, or a view?

8. What is the minimum number of square feet you would find acceptable?

9. What are your needs as far as outdoor space? Are you excited about gardening, or do you prefer to have your yard maintained by someone else?

10. Do you need a garage? If so, how many spaces would be ideal? Do you need to be close to public transportation?

11. Do you prefer a single-story home or are two or more stories acceptable? Are there any other accessibility requirements, such as ramps or wider doorways? What about baby safety?

12. Do you want a home with a pool and/or spa?

13. Are you open to viewing homes that might need renovation or cosmetic updating? If so, how much work are you willing to undertake?

14. Do you expect to have laundry facilities in your home, or in the case of some condos, are community laundry facilities acceptable? For in-home facilities, do you need a separate room, or is the garage or basement an acceptable location?

15. Do you need to be in a particular school district? Do you need to be within walking distance to shops and restaurants?

16. Are you comfortable with a property that has a homeowners' association? What are the maximum monthly HOA dues you would consider? What about paying Mello-Roos fees (see Glossary)?

By answering these questions, not only will you be looking at the homes best suited for you, but your real estate agent will be able to determine whether or not your expectations are realistic and provide you with guidance if not.

## The Second Step: Looking at Houses

**The second step** is the fun part: Looking at houses! The process can be a bit overwhelming, especially for a first-time buyer, so here are some tips that will help keep you focused and on the path towards homeownership:

**Be clear about your budget and stick to it.** It's okay to look at homes that are slightly above what you want to spend, as there is often the opportunity to negotiate a lower price. However, be aware that in today's competitive market, most properties receive multiple offers, and sellers may not need to discount their prices. Your maximum budget should equal the size of the payment you are *comfortable* paying each month, not necessarily the max for which you have qualified.

**Location, location, location.** The location of your home not only helps determine price, it is a huge factor in your daily life. For instance, buying in a more outlying area means that you will likely get more for your money, but are you prepared for the added commute time? And what about the neighborhood itself? It may seem calm and quiet at 11:00 a.m. when everyone is at work, but what about Saturday night? Does it turn into party central? It is always a good idea to visit a neighborhood in the evening and on the weekend before buying. Walk around and talk to people and try to get a real feel for what it would be like to live there.

**Age matters.** There is nothing wrong with buying an older home. In fact, in many areas, there are numerous benefits, such as larger lots and character details. However, when viewing an older home, pay close attention to big-ticket items. How old is the roof? Do the windows need to be replaced? Is the electric panel updated and capable of handling the load of all of today's appliances? Are the furnace and water heater on their last legs? Items that will need to be replaced or updated shouldn't necessarily be a deal breaker, but they should be taken into consideration in terms of the price you offer and the funds you will need to complete the work.

**Look at the bones, not the makeup.** Buyers may be swayed by the way a home is decorated, which is why homes are often staged. For instance, did you ever notice that in model homes all the interior doors are removed to help make the rooms feel larger? The use of mirrors, lighting, and the strategic arrangement of furniture is often used to give a home the sense of being move-in ready. What you need to look at, though, is the flow and size of the rooms, and how well it fits your lifestyle. For instance, if you love to entertain, a home with no space for a dining table might not be a good option. Or, there might not be a logical place to put your big-screen TV. The opposite situation is also a problem. If a home is a cluttered mess, dirty, or poorly decorated, it may be hard to visualize living there. Focus on the layout, not the color of the walls or the things filling the space. And remember, moving walls and remodeling kitchens are expensive!

**Take pictures and notes.** As you enter a property, take a picture of the address. If you do that first, you will know that the pictures that follow are of that particular property. Your real estate agent should provide you with a printed flyer for each property you visit. As you view a home, take notes on the back of the flyer about things that stand out for you, both positive and negative features, and take a photo. That way, you have both pictures and notes to review later. This is especially important if viewing several homes in one day. The various attributes of one property versus another can all swim together in your head. To help you keep everything organized, please see the House-Hunting Checklist in the Appendix.

**Rein in your emotions.** Don't get me wrong, selecting a home to buy is a very emotional experience, with a large number of people saying they just "knew" the minute they walked in the door. Getting a good vibe from a home is important, but try to specifically identify what it is that has you feeling so ready to commit, and then balance that against your "must-have" list. It may be the kitchen of your dreams, but the family room is too small to be practical. The view is breathtaking, but the location will add an extra hour a day to your commute. An experienced listing agent will make sure the marketing and staging focus on the best features of the property. Just make sure you stay focused on everything that will make this the best *livable* choice for you.

**No home is perfect.** Be prepared to compromise on something. Unless you are building a custom-designed home in your dream location, there will likely be something about the home you buy that is not quite perfect. *The important thing is to know the difference between what you must have and what you can live without.*

For instance, if you must have a separate bedroom for each of your kids, that should not be an area of compromise. However, if you find a home that is almost perfect, but it doesn't have a fireplace or walk-in closet, those might be things you could do without in order to get everything else on your list.

## The Third Step: Writing Your Offer

*The third step* is to write your offer ASAP! In this competitive market, if you find the home that's right for you, write your offer *immediately*, as there will likely be multiple offers. *Remember, it is much easier to get out of a deal than to get into one!* And as you'll learn later in this book, you are generally protected against losing your deposit during your inspection period. So go for it!

SAVVY SHOPPER TIPS: Be clear about what you need and what you want. If buying with a spouse, family member, or friend, make sure you have a very candid discussion about which features or attributes could become a deal maker or breaker. Be organized in your house hunting. Make the effort to take notes and photos. If there are properties that are a definite "no," put them aside in a separate folder to help you stay focused. It is advisable to write offers on more than one property at a time. Better to be in the position of choosing between two accepted offers than not even in the game!

# CHAPTER 8

## DREAM HOME OR NIGHTMARE? THE PROS AND CONS OF BUYING A SHORT SALE OR FORECLOSURE

*Back in 2009, I was working with a couple looking to purchase a home with enough room for an extra garage, as the husband loved to fix up old cars. I located a property that had been foreclosed and was now owned by the bank. It had been sitting on the market for a while, as the home's design was rather taste-specific and not everyone's cup of tea. My buyers were okay with the house (he was more interested in the generous lot size and huge parking area and she rather fancied all the archways), so we wrote an offer that was quickly accepted.*

*The property was not sewer connected, being in a slightly rural area, so as part of their due diligence, my buyers ordered a septic inspection. What a surprise when no septic tank cap could be located! The bank, of course, had no knowledge of the property, so the only way we could discover the location of the septic tank was for the septic technician to trace a signal on a device he flushed down the toilet. When the sensor tracked the beacon, we discovered that the previous owner had poured a driveway over the top of the sep-*

*tic tank—totally in code violation. Not only should a septic tank not be located under a driveway, they'd also covered access, so there wasn't even any way to pump it!*

*What a mess! In order to make the house livable and to code, the concrete over the tank would have to be removed, the tank relocated and installed, and new concrete poured to re-route the driveway. The quote was $30,000! We were at an impasse. The bank did not want to pay to have all of this work completed, and the buyers didn't have an extra $30,000 to complete the work, even if the bank lowered the price. Plus, the lender for my buyer's new loan would not lend the money without the septic tank clearance.*

*We went back and forth with the bank trying to resolve the issue. I knew the bank was in a tough spot because now that they had the report and knew about the septic issue, they were legally bound to disclose the information to any potential buyer, and all they wanted to do was get the deal closed and off their books.*

*I finally suggested a compromise: The bank would pay to have the concrete removed covering the septic tank and pay to have a new one installed in an approved location, with permits. This would be sufficient to satisfy my buyer's lender. The bank would also reduce the price of the home by $10,000, and my buyers would take on the responsibility of pouring a new driveway after close of escrow. Whew!*

E ven though the number of distressed properties on the market has diminished considerably over the past three years, short sales and bank-owned properties are available in most areas, and they still hold appeal for many buyers. Depending on the area and condition of the home, distressed properties typically sell for about 10% under market value, making them especially attractive to investors and buyers looking for a good deal.

## The Short Sale

A short sale occurs when the proceeds from the sale of the home are insufficient to pay off the mortgage(s) and closing costs, and the bank agrees to accept a reduced payoff. Often, the seller of the home has fallen behind on payments, and their only option to avoid foreclosure is to try to sell the home as a short sale, which is less detrimental to their credit.

From a buyer's perspective, the biggest difference between a traditional sale and a short sale is that the seller is not the decision-maker. The seller and their agent will determine which offer seems most favorable, and that offer will be submitted to the bank (or banks, if there is a second mortgage as well). It is then up to the bank(s) to decide if the purchase will be allowed.

This decision-making process can take anywhere from 30 to 120 days or more, and in the end, the sale still might not be approved. If there are two mortgages, it becomes even more difficult, as the second lien holder, being in the junior position, is not entitled to anything if there are insufficient proceeds to pay off the first lien. They must rely on the good graces of the first lien holder to offer them a token payoff, usually between $3,000-$15,000. If they want to play hardball, the second lien holder can block the approval and/or demand a higher payoff. Thus, time and uncertainty are the largest obstacles in a short sale.

The biggest drawback to a short sale is that you really have no idea about whether or not your offer will be approved, or how long it might take. The other negative is that a financially stressed seller is not in a position to make any repairs, and the bank, which is already losing money, will not agree to any repairs, so you really are purchasing the property "as-is."

## REO Foreclosures

A real estate owned (or REO) property is one that has been foreclosed by the bank but did not sell at auction, so title reverted back to the bank. Banks are not in the business of selling homes, so they turn over the task of unloading the inventory to asset management companies, who in turn assign the listings to local agents who specialize in selling REOs. Unlike short sales, the decision-making process is usually quicker. The asset manager knows the parameters of what the bank is willing to accept, so even though the final decision must come from the bank, the asset manager can negotiate and respond in a timely manner.

The biggest drawback to purchasing a bank-owned property is that the owner (the bank) has never lived in the property, or even set foot in the home, and thus has no knowledge of anything about the property. They are exempt from supplying most disclosures; whereas in a short sale, the sellers have lived in the property, and even if they can't pay for repairs, they are legally required to disclose all known facts about the home. Buyer beware! Often, foreclosed homes have been neglected or even abused by their former owners, who were angry about the foreclosure. Make sure you conduct all necessary investigations and are satisfied with the condition of the property. What you don't know could prove to be a very costly discovery!

So if you're looking for a deal, a short sale or REO might be a good choice if you're not in a hurry to complete the purchase, are prepared for the offer to be rejected, are willing to accept responsibility for all investigations, and don't mind purchasing the home "as-is."

SAVVY SHOPPER TIPS: If you're interested in short sales or REO properties, your real estate agent can perform a search specific to those parameters. If this is their area of expertise, they might also be able to access data for homeowners who are behind on their mortgage, but for whom a Notice of Default has not yet been filed. These homeowners might be interested in an off-market short sale. Always do complete inspections. $500-$1000 spent on investigating the property could save you thousands. Be prepared to walk away if the necessary repairs are too great for the price.

# CHAPTER 9
## HOW TO MAKE AN OFFER THEY CAN'T REFUSE

*There is an art to writing a compelling offer, which is another reason to work with an experienced real estate agent. Personally, when acting as a listing agent, I love to receive a well put together offer, as it makes my job much easier when I present the offer to my client, the seller. For instance, we like to see that all of the appropriate documents for the particular sales situation are included and completed properly; the language in any addendum clearly states the buyer position or request; and, hopefully, there is a cover letter that explains a bit about why the buyer wants to buy this particular property. What a listing agent never wants is to have to call the buyer's agent and ask for missing documents, such as proof of funds or a loan pre-approval.*

*That being said, I need to share a little story here.*

*On January 1st, I listed a lovely condo in a very popular area. The response was immediate, and we had several showings scheduled the first day, despite it being New Year's Day. By the second day, we had an offer, which we countered the following day, almost at the top of our price range. We really thought the buy-*

*er would counter back with a lower number, but the following afternoon, January 4th, they accepted our counter and all parties executed the contract. I then moved the listing to pending status in the MLS late that night.*

*Fast-forward to the morning of January 5th, and I receive another equally strong offer. The agent had not checked the MLS to see that it was no longer an active listing. When I spoke to him, he mentioned they would have had their offer in on the 3rd, but they were waiting for an updated pre-approval letter.*

*Timing is everything! Had they submitted the offer earlier, they might have had a chance, as we would have countered both parties. And even if they didn't submit it on the 3rd, if the agent had contacted me and said they would have an offer over to me in the next 24 hours, I probably would have advised my clients to wait and see how the second offer looked before sealing the deal with the original buyer.*

After all the planning, searching, and viewing of homes which didn't quite make the grade, you've found the house you want to buy. It's time to write an offer, but where do you begin?

## Writing Your Offer

There are five things you'll want to consider when writing your offer.

1. **Determine value.** The starting point is determining the value of your selected property. Your real estate

agent will review comparable sales from the past six or 12 months, depending on the level of activity in your market. Generally speaking, in most cities, appraisers will only accept values for sales going back six months. Your appraiser will try to find properties as similar to the one you have selected as possible, matching number of bedrooms and baths, square footage, lot size, and age. They will also look at other attributes, such as views, age of the roof and windows, and whether or not any of the rooms have been remodeled.

2. **Set your price.** Once you've determined the fair market value of your chosen home, you need to determine an offer price. This will depend on several factors, including the level of competition, how long the home has been on the market, the seller's motivation, and how you plan to purchase the home. For instance, if the seller has had the property listed for 60 days and has already made an offer on their next home, they need to sell quickly, and you might be able to offer less than if the property had only been listed for five days and the seller was in no hurry to move. Likewise, if you are asking the seller to pay for closing costs, be prepared to offer more than if you were asking for no concessions. (See Chapter 11 for more information on closing costs.)

One thing to keep in mind is that it is fine to start with an offer that is under market value, but if you come in too low, you risk insulting the seller to the point that they don't even want to counter. In California, a seller who has listed their home with what is called "value range pricing," such as

$450,000-$500,000, does not have to respond to an offer that is below the low end of the range. Also, in a competitive market where the seller is receiving multiple offers, it may be best to come in *above* asking price, if you really want the house and your agent feels that it would appraise at your offered price. However, when offering above market value, you run the risk of the appraisal coming in too low. This means you'll either need to renegotiate the sales price, pay the difference out of pocket, or move on to another property after having paid for an appraisal, which is generally $350-$500 or more. Learn more about how to handle appraisal issues in Chapter 16.

3. **Determine your deposit.** You will also have to determine the size of your earnest money deposit. This is around 1–3% of the offered price and will be deposited to the escrow holder generally within three days of acceptance of your offer. (More about escrow in Chapter 12.) For some loan types—such as VA, which offers 100% financing—the initial deposit might be less, or in some cases, when you want the seller to see the level of your commitment, the deposit might be more. Historically, the earnest money deposit was made payable to the broker who deposited it in a trust account. The broker would then write a check to the escrow holder when an offer was accepted. However, today's brokers are less inclined to manage client funds and are more likely to just include a copy of the check from the buyer, payable to escrow with the offer, or include no check copy at all.

4. **Sign the documents.** Your agent will prepare all of the documents for you to sign, which may include a

special addendum if the property is held in a trust, is in probate, or is a short sale or REO. In California, the standardized form used to submit an offer is the Residential Purchase Agreement. Once signed by all parties, this offer becomes the actual purchase contract and is submitted to escrow for fulfillment of the transaction. *If this is your first time writing an offer, please ask your agent to sit down with you and walk you through each section of the contract to make sure you understand and agree to all of the terms and conditions.* If you have written several offers and are familiar with the content, your agent may use an electronic signing service, such as DocuSign, which allows you to sign in just minutes from your computer, phone, or tablet.

5. **Submit your offer.** The next step is the actual submission of your offer. In today's age of electronic communication, most listing agents request that offers be submitted via email. This also cuts down on wasted paper. Along with the offer, your agent will include a copy of your loan pre-approval and a bank or other financial statement which shows that you have sufficient funds to cover your down payment and closing costs. In some areas of the country, the buyer still submits an actual check payable to the listing brokerage for the earnest money deposit. As nearly all submissions in California are electronic, there are fewer and fewer brokers accepting earnest money deposit funds. Often an agent will include a copy of the earnest money deposit check, but more likely it is just noted on the offer that, upon acceptance, the buyer will deliver or wire the deposit to escrow within three days.

To gain an edge over your competition, and depending on the situation, you may want to request that your agent also includes a cover letter, telling the seller a bit of your story. For instance, if the sellers are selling the home where they raised their children to adulthood, they might like to think that another young couple would want to do the same. Or maybe share a bit about your volunteer work and why you want to be in that particular neighborhood. It's even okay to include a photo of you or your family. On the other hand, if it's an investor selling, looking to maximize his return on a rental property, a letter will likely have little impact. It is the responsibility of the listing agent to make sure that their seller has not specified that they only want to see offers from a particular sex, religion, race, ethnic group, or any other group that might raise Equal Housing Opportunity issues.

Once your offer is submitted, make sure your agent receives confirmation of receipt, as different email programs will sometimes recognize an offer as spam and put it in the trash file. Unless you have offered on a short sale or REO, in California, you should hear back from the listing agent within three days with either a rejection or a written counteroffer, unless a faster response time was otherwise indicated in the offer.

## Should You Write Multiple Offers?

So, you've just put in an offer on a home and you're waiting to hear back. What next? Depending on the market, you might want to consider putting in an offer on another home in the meantime. This is especially true in a highly competitive market, or if you know there are multiple offers on the home you hope to purchase. *Remember, it is always easier to get out of a deal than to get into one!*

## Should You Write a "Blind" Offer?

Writing an offer on a property you haven't viewed is referred to as a *blind offer*. Blind offers are generally written in markets where the inventory of available homes is low and you have many buyers vying for the same property. Often, buyers will write an offer as soon as a home comes on the market, just to have a chance. So, what is the risk in writing an offer without seeing the property first?

In my opinion, the only real risk is that you might overpay. As long as you don't remove inspection contingencies from your offer, it is not difficult to cancel a contract if you are dissatisfied with the property once you see it. While having many photos and even video will give you a good idea of what the home looks like, there are many things you can only assess by physically viewing the property. For instance, the photos probably won't show an outdated A/C unit or pool heater on its last legs, or the unexplained stain on the ceiling. Writing an offer based solely on comparable sales means that, in a competitive situation where you know there will be multiple offers, you are likely to write a higher offer than you might have had you viewed the property and been able to take into consideration any necessary repairs.

That being said, there is usually the opportunity to negotiate repairs after a home inspection. So, I say if you're in a hot market with limited inventory, go for it! If you see a listing online and think it might be "the one," write that offer, NOW! There is no upfront financial risk in submitting an offer, and waiting several days until you can view the property may put you out of the running.

## *Writing a Contingent Offer*

Maybe you're ready to move up to a larger home, or perhaps you want to change neighborhoods and you need to sell your current home in order to have sufficient money to purchase the next one. This gets tricky. Do you sell your current home before shopping for another and risk having to make an interim move into a rental, or do you shop for a new home and hope your current property sells in time to make the deal work?

Writing an offer on a new home while yours still needs to sell is referred to as a *contingent offer*. The purchase is contingent on your home selling, and depending on your market, this can be a difficult offer to get accepted. If you look at it from a seller's point of view, if they receive two fairly equal offers, one contingent and one not, it's likely they will accept the non-contingent offer, as it's a cleaner deal with less likelihood of falling apart.

If you're going to write a contingent offer, at least have your home on the market, and preferably in escrow. This may be sufficient to satisfy the sellers, especially if their property has been on the market for some time. On the other hand, if you are in a highly competitive market where every listing is getting multiple offers, your chances of getting a contingent offer accepted are slim to none. In this case, it would probably make more sense to sell first, move into a month-to-month rental, and put most of your belongings in storage so you're able to write a non-contingent offer.

SAVVY SHOPPER TIPS: In a competitive market where housing inventory is low, be prepared to pay actual market value, or even slightly more. On the other hand, if inventory is high, it is a buyer's market, and it's much more likely you'll be able to purchase for lower than asking price. If offering above asking price, make sure you know how you'll handle the additional cost before writing the offer. Whether this is your first offer or your tenth, review the key items, including price, down payment, and contingency periods before signing. Discuss with your real estate agent about making multiple and/or blind offers to improve your chances in a competitive market. If you find a property you like, don't sleep on it or call in all the relatives for their opinion. Just write the darn offer!

Also, if you know you are going to write an offer on a particular property, have your real estate agent contact the listing agent and let them know when to expect it. They might be ready to make a decision, and you'll be out of the running unless they know you will also be submitting an offer. You snooze you lose!

# CHAPTER 10
## NEGOTIATION
### HOW TO TURN AN OFFER INTO A DEAL

*Several years ago, I was representing a buyer who was looking to purchase a home in one of the most exclusive and expensive neighborhoods in San Diego. He was in a great position, as he was prepared to pay up to $1.8 million—all cash. We looked at quite a few properties before he settled on a grand home with over 7,000 square feet and a phenomenal view. It was offered at $1.75 million, so it was definitely within budget.*

*The home had been a foreclosure that the current owner bought at auction just two months earlier for $1.4 million. Even though the house was just a few years old, there were some minor repairs needed, which the new owner took care of shortly after purchase.*

*Knowing what the seller had paid for the property just two months earlier, and knowing how minor the repairs had been, my buyer was not inclined to offer anything above $1.5 million—despite the fact that the list price of $1.75 million really was market value.*

*So, we submitted an offer at $1.5 million, all cash, with a 15-day close of escrow—certainly an attractive offer given that this was when the market had hit bottom, and there was a scarcity of buyers for houses in this price range.*

*The seller countered us at $1.65 million, and we countered at $1.55 million. We were now just $100,000 off, so I figured we would eventually meet in the middle and my buyer would get the home. The seller came down another $40,000 to $1.61 million, and my buyer responded back with a $40,000 increase to $1.59 million. They were now just $20,000 apart! And then, the negotiation stopped. The seller refused to come down any lower, and my buyer refused to come up, even another $10,000! The seller was intent on squeezing every possible dollar out of the place, and my buyer was equally intent on getting a steal of a deal. So, despite my best efforts to have these two stubborn men see the value in just a little more compromise, the deal fell apart.*

*The big house sat on the market for another four months before the seller accepted an offer for $1.5 million; $90,000 less than my buyer's final offer! In the meantime, my buyer decided to rent a large home for a year, which was certainly disappointing for me! His rental was in the same neighborhood, but not nearly as elegant as the home he had tried to buy. When I checked back with him several months later, I learned that he had negotiated with the owner of the property he was renting and purchased directly from him for $1.65 million—$60,000 more than his highest offer for the better property!*

## *Your Offer Has Been Submitted*

You've done your homework and written an offer that you hope will be well-received. Your agent has submitted it and confirmed receipt, and now you wait for a response according to the time frame specified in your offer, which is generally 1–3 days.

But a million questions swarm through your head: *Did I offer too little to be competitive? Did I offer too much? How many other offers has the seller received? Should I have waived certain contingencies? Do I really need a termite clearance?*

Whoa! Settle down. The game is just beginning. The whole idea is to get your foot in the door with an initial offer that is attractive enough to get you to the next round. I should add that occasionally there is a situation where an offer is so stellar the seller accepts it without countering. But generally, whether or not there is more than one offer, a seller will counter to see how they can negotiate their best deal.

## *Receiving the Counteroffer*

If you've received a counteroffer, congratulations! You're in the game. The first thing you need to realize is that almost everything in a real estate transaction is negotiable, and the key to success is based on several factors:

1. *Be prepared! Learn as much as you can about the seller's motivation and situation.* This is your real estate agent's job. The more you know about what the seller is looking for, the better you can respond to their counteroffer. It makes a big difference if you know that the seller owns the property free and clear, versus having only 10% equity. Or, if the seller is relocating

and needs a quick sale, you'll have better leverage than if you're dealing with a seller who's in no hurry.

2. *You may be one of several buyers being countered, and it is likely that each counter is slightly different, depending on the original offer.* You may also be asked to respond with your "highest and best" offer, indicating that the seller has multiple offers and doesn't want to go through several rounds of counters. In either situation, you need to figure out how to sweeten your offer, and as I describe in the next section, it isn't just about the money. However, if you know that you're in a multiple-offer situation and the seller has countered at a specific price, you might beat your competition by simply offering $500 more than the seller's counter.

3. *Understand your own parameters and stick to them.* If $450,000 is the absolute max you can afford comfortably, you cannot accept a $480,000 counter. You must know when to sweeten your offer, hold, or just walk away.

## Just What Is Negotiable?

As noted earlier, almost everything is negotiable, so don't get fixated on the price. For many sellers, price is just a part of the equation. Ask yourself, "What can I offer that will be attractive to the seller while still allowing me to get the best deal?" Most negotiations involve a certain amount of compromise and concession on both sides. The goal is for the seller to sell and the buyer to buy, each feeling like the transaction was fair to both parties.

Here are a few negotiable items, other than price, to consider:

- **Seller concessions.** If a seller is considering two offers, and one requests a $5K contribution to buyer closing costs and the other does not, it is pretty clear which has an advantage.

- **Earnest money deposit.** A larger or increased deposit generally demonstrates that you are a serious buyer.

- **Escrow time frame.** Would the seller favor a longer or shorter escrow? If going for less than 30 days and you're financing the purchase, make sure that is a realistic expectation for your lender.

- **Service providers.** Often times, a seller will have a specific escrow or title company they prefer to work with.

- **Seller rent-back.** Perhaps the seller needs to rent back the house from you for a month while closing escrow on their next home.

- **Seller financing.** Often sellers like the idea of carrying back a small second mortgage. Or conversely, he or she may want all of their money out of the deal.

- **Contingencies.** Be careful about removing contingencies for inspection of the property. Buyer beware! You need adequate time to satisfy yourself about the condition of the property, but shortening the inspection period might be seen as favorable by the seller.

- **Fees.** There are many fees involved in a real estate transaction, including transfer tax, escrow, title insurance, and HOA transfer fees and docs. Offering to pay a fee that might traditionally be paid by the seller may put your offer in a stronger position.

- **Personal property.** This can work both ways. In one transaction, it might be better not to ask for the new appliances as part of the deal, while in another, allowing the sellers to leave an old refrigerator or piano might be doing them a favor.

- **Repairs.** Depending on the condition of the property, who pays for repairs can be an item for negotiation. However, be realistic about costs, time, and your skill set. As the saying goes, "Don't bite off more than you can chew." Also, be aware of any lender-required repairs and who is allowed to pay for what, particularly with VA or FHA loans. Your loan officer should be consulted regarding required repairs for the type of loan you are getting.

- **Home warranty.** While purchasing a home warranty is advisable, it doesn't necessarily mean that the seller should pay for it. Perhaps the buyer, their agent, or for first-time buyers, maybe their parents would like to buy it? There are many providers of home warranties that range in price from about $300-$1000, depending on the size of the home and the coverage.

*Before we wrap up this section, I'd like to share another personal story. This one is about the negotiation my current husband, Ronn, and I did while shopping for our first home together.*

*We began our home search in September 2001, but then came 9/11, and everything was put on hold. The whole country was frozen in uncertainty, but we decided to resume our search at the start of October.*

*We quickly found a home that was perfect for us! It was a fixer, but the layout of the home was great and the location was ideal. The house had been on the market for a couple of months. The owner was in an assisted living home, and the home was being sold by his children to help pay for his care. I believe they were asking $389,000, which was a little bit high, considering that everything in the house was terribly dated. We really wanted the house, so we offered $349,000, which was really about as high as we could go at that time. They countered at $375,000. We took a deep breath and decided we couldn't really go any higher and just walked away.*

*Two weeks later, the house was still on the market, and the seller's kids were getting nervous. With all of the confusion caused by 9/11, the real estate market had come to a virtual standstill. No one was buying or selling. We took advantage of the uncertainty and decided to re-submit our $349,000 offer. Not knowing when another offer would come along, the seller accepted our offer, and we ended up with a great deal without overpaying. Our walking away and then coming back left the seller far more motivated and ready to make a deal.*

## What to Do When It Comes Down to Price

Often, a negotiation will go back and forth with counteroffers, arriving at agreement on all terms except the price. This usually occurs for one of three reasons:

1. The seller has unrealistic expectations about the value of their home.

2. Inventory is low, and the market is so competitive that the seller is hoping to drive up the price through a bidding war.

3. The buyer wants a great deal and refuses to pay market price.

The most important piece of information you'll need at this point is a clear picture of the property's *actual market value*. Prior to writing your offer, your real estate agent should have provided you with comparable active and sold listings. Before increasing your offer, it's a good idea to have your real estate agent check the comps again to see if there are any new listings or closings that will affect market value one way or the other.

If after reviewing the comps you and your real estate agent determine that the seller's price is still above market value, you have several choices:

1. You can hold at your price and hope that no one else will bid higher. If the market is not competitive, this might mean waiting a couple of weeks for the seller to agree.

2. You can just pay the extra money out of pocket and consider it a premium you paid to get the house you really want.

3. Depending on the dollar amount of the gap between your offer and the seller's price, you can increase your offer by slightly more than 50% of the difference, which might be enough to let the seller feel like they won.

4. You can agree to the higher price, but with the condition that you will not pay more than the actual appraised value.

> SAVVY SHOPPER TIPS: Negotiation is not just about price. Make sure you are exploring all options that might be favorable to you and/or the seller. Don't be afraid to walk away for a few days, or even longer, depending on how competitive the market is. Be clear in your mind about what part of your offer is not negotiable and what other terms might have some room for flexibility. Every successful negotiation includes compromise. Don't be blinded by your own need to be right or to win to the extent that you lose the whole deal.

# CHAPTER 11
## WHO PAYS FOR WHAT
## WHEN BUYING A HOME?

*A few years ago, a young woman came to me hoping to buy her first home. She had a job as a corporate attorney and had been with the firm for over two years. Armed with a well-paying job and great credit, she was pre-approved and ready to buy. The only problem was, with over $40,000 in student loan debt to pay, she hadn't been able to save as much as she would have liked for a down payment and closing costs. In fact, she only had $10,000 saved and didn't really want to spend every penny and leave herself with no cushion.*

*We found a local credit union that offered 100% financing for people with great credit and she qualified. They also had low closing costs, which we knew would be important.*

*After looking for about two weeks, we found the perfect condo, and she was ready to write an offer. However, before doing so, I worked up a cost sheet for her and estimated that her total closing costs would be around $8,750. That was just cutting it too close, and she was starting to think that she'd have to wait until she could save more money.*

*I suggested we ask the sellers for help. The property was listed at $345,000, which was slightly under market value, but the sellers needed a quick closing. We offered $350,000 and asked for a seller credit of $5,000 to help pay her closing costs. Her offer was accepted, and 30 days later she was a happy homeowner. Her payments were slightly higher than if she had bought the condo for $345,000 or less, but she could afford the payment, and she still had some money in the bank for a rainy day.*

B uying a piece of property is not a simple transaction, and buyers are often surprised by the number of parties involved, who of course all need to be paid. But how is it determined who pays for what? What is a seller expense, and what will you, the buyer, need to pay?

Interestingly, who pays for what is often based on regional or state customs. My company, Steele Group Realty, is based in San Diego County, so we'll examine expenses for a typical Southern California purchase transaction using the Residential Purchase Agreement developed by the California Association of REALTORS and an ALTA Final Settlement Statement as our guide. Typical closing costs in Southern California run 2–5% of the sales price. Understanding who pays for what, and even who chooses the different service providers, will vary from state to state and should be discussed with your real estate agent prior to writing an offer.

## Inspections and Reports

Typically, the seller pays for a Natural Hazard Disclosure (NHD) Report delivered to the buyer by a third-party provider. The NHD Report discloses known information about potential hazards or conditions surrounding the location of the property being purchased (more on this and other disclosures in Chapter 15). Often, a buyer will also request a C.L.U.E. (Comprehensive Loss Underwriting Exchange) Report that reveals past insurance claims on the property. The C.L.U.E. Report can only be ordered by the homeowner. The seller will also generally be responsible for paying for a termite and wood-destroying pest inspection and report. As the buyer, you would pay for a general home inspection, unless the seller paid for an inspection prior to listing the home, in which case you may still want to pay for a second inspection. You would also pay for any other specialized inspections, such roofing, plumbing, or electrical inspections. If there is a well or septic system on the property, it is usually up to the seller to have those systems inspected and certified. On a large property, you may also want a survey that marks the corners of the lot. This may or may not be paid by the seller. Keep in mind, *just because one party pays for an inspection does not mean they will pay for any repairs that might be necessary as a result of that inspection.* Repairs are subsequently negotiated between the buyer and seller.

## Government Requirements

There are certain minimum state and local safety requirements that must be met prior to close of escrow, unless the seller is exempt. Generally, the seller is required to pay for the installation of smoke and carbon monoxide detectors as required by California law. The seller is also responsible for the correct water heater bracing to protect against tipping in an earthquake. If there are other minimum safety standards that must be met, the seller is generally responsible for those expenses.

## Escrow and Title Insurance

In California, most real estate transfers are managed by escrow companies, not lawyers as they are in many parts of the country. Escrow companies are neutral third parties, licensed to manage the accounting and accurate distribution of the funds of both the buyer and seller (more on escrow in the following chapter). As such, both sides of the transaction are charged for the services of the escrow company. It is customary for buyers and sellers to each pay their own escrow fees, or to split the total fee 50/50. Escrow fees are based on the sales price of the property.

Title insurance is designed to protect both the new owner and lender from financial loss due to title defects, liens, or other title-related issues. The seller generally pays for the owner's title policy, and the buyer pays for a title insurance policy to protect the lender if the purchase is being financed.

## Taxes and Fees

In California, there is a transfer tax paid to the county when real estate title is transferred. Throughout most of the state, that tax is $1.10 per $1,000 of the purchase price. This is generally paid by the seller. Information about transfer taxes in other states is generally available from your agent or the local assessor's office. Property taxes are prorated to the date of closing and are paid by the buyer and seller accordingly.

If the property has a homeowners' association (HOA), the association charges a transfer fee as well as a fee for providing all of the HOA documents to the buyer. The preparation of certain HOA documents is required by law to be paid by the seller, and, in most cases, the seller pays for all fees associated with the HOA transfer.

## Home Warranties

A home warranty protects the buyer against certain defects or failures in the home's systems for 12–13 months after close of escrow. Policies vary considerably as far as what is covered and the cost of a service call. Home warranties are not a part of every transaction, and who pays for a home warranty is definitely negotiable.

## Commissions

Commissions paid to real estate brokers are generally paid by the seller. Commissions in California are negotiable, but generally range from 5–6% of the sales price, normally split equally between the listing broker (the seller's broker) and the buyer's broker. The brokers then pay the agents a percentage of the commission based on their contractual agreement with the broker.

## Other Buyer Expenses

There are other expenses you will incur that are associated with your new home loan, including an appraisal fee, loan origination fee, notary fee, recording charges, an underwriting and loan processing fee, and a credit report fee. Depending on your loan type and lender, some of these loan-related expenses may be wrapped into the loan. The buyer will also pay for hazard insurance. Most lenders will require the annual premium to be paid in full (more on insurance in Chapter 17). Your escrow officer might also add a pad or contingency fund of several hundred dollars just to make sure there are sufficient funds to close in case closing is delayed or there is an unexpected fee or expense. Any unspent portion of the pad will be refunded to you after closing.

## *Seller Concessions*

Despite what is usual and customary regarding allocation of costs, it is not unusual for the seller to pay some of the buyer's closing costs. This is especially true if the buyer is using a VA loan, where he or she may not be allowed to pay for certain items. The seller may also provide a closing cost concession if the buyer agrees to pay a slightly higher price. This is advantageous if you, as the buyer, are short on immediate funds but well qualified for a higher loan amount. You are basically just financing some of your closing costs (like we saw in the opening story of this chapter).

SAVVY SHOPPER TIPS: Who pays for what is largely negotiable. Make sure that you discuss allocation of costs with your real estate agent when writing your offer. They can also provide you with a cost estimate before you even write an offer. Escrow and title insurance fees do not vary widely from one company to another, but depending on which party selects the service providers, it may be worthwhile to get a quote from at least two companies. Loan fees are definitely worth shopping, and be sure to ask your lender if you can wrap certain fees into the loan. Some credit unions have very low costs, and some banks may have reduced fees for banking customers. Most important: Ask your escrow officer or lawyer for an explanation of any fees you don't understand.

# CHAPTER 12
## ALL ABOUT ESCROW
## AND WHY IT'S IMPORTANT

*As I sat down to write this chapter, I realized that I don't have any dramatic stories about escrows, and that's likely because I've worked with the same escrow officer for over 10 years. Whenever I'm the listing agent, I always encourage my clients to work with her. I've followed her to three different companies and will continue to follow her should she move again. The degree of responsibility and detail required in her position would make most people crazy. But I know that I can always count on her to be accurate and on time. She is patient and caring and always ready to explain items to my clients. If your real estate agent has a favorite escrow officer, work with them. It is likely that they too will provide great service.*

You and the seller have finally come to agreement on the terms under which you'll purchase your dream home, but now what? How can both parties be sure that everything in the purchase contract actually happens? Assuring that all terms of the written agreement are fulfilled is the job of a neutral third party referred to as the escrow holder. In some states, this job is handled by an attorney, but in California, it is customary for the escrow to be handled by an escrow or title company.

## *About Escrow Companies*

Companies providing escrow services are regulated by state law and are broken into two categories of regulation: independent or non-independent. *Non-independent* escrow providers include attorneys, savings and loan institutions, real estate brokers, and title companies—all of which are governed by specific regulatory organizations. *Independent* escrow companies have no other business interests other than supplying escrow services, and they are licensed by the California Department of Business Oversight.

Deciding which escrow provider to use is part of the negotiation process. In today's competitive market, the buyer will often include in the offer that selection of escrow and title services are "seller's choice," thus appearing to grant a concession to the seller right up front. In reality, prices charged by the various companies for escrow services do not vary tremendously and are negotiable to a certain extent, so selecting the escrow provider is usually more important to the agents than the buyers and sellers. As it is against the law for a real estate agent to accept any type of gift or fee for referring an escrow company, or any other service provider for that matter, it really comes down to quality of service. Most agents, when given the opportunity, will encourage their clients to use a particular company and escrow officer based on their prior positive experience in working with that company and officer.

## *Opening Escrow*

Escrow is generally opened by the listing agent, who will email the selected escrow officer a copy of the fully executed Residential Purchase Agreement and any other documents that are incorporated into the agreement, such as counteroffers and any addenda. The listing agent will also indicate which title insurance company is selected and provide the following information:

- Phone numbers and postal and email addresses for the sellers.

- Contact information for the buyer's agent.

- A copy of the pre-approval letter if the purchase is to be financed. The letter will have contact information for the lender.

- HOA contact information if applicable.

- Commission information as stated in the listing agreement and MLS.

- If the buyer has provided an earnest money deposit check payable to the listing broker, the listing broker will write a check from his or her trust account payable to the escrow company.

The escrow period is stipulated in the Residential Purchase Agreement and is generally 30 days for a transaction involving a new first mortgage; longer in the case of a short sale or probate sale, and often much shorter in an all-cash transaction. In certain circumstances, with the agreement of both parties, the escrow period can be extended beyond the agreed upon date of closing.

Generally, within the first three days, the buyer will deposit their earnest money by check or wire transfer. During this time period, the escrow officer will also send draft escrow instructions to both agents, who will review the key terms of the transaction. Upon approval from the agents, the escrow officer will send escrow instructions to both the buyers and sellers, including several forms that must be completed and returned.

One of the most important forms is the Statement of Information or Statement of Identity. This questionnaire asks for very complete personal information about marital, job, and residence history, which may seem a bit intrusive. However, it is very important to provide complete information to make certain that your identity is not confused with someone else who might have a similar name or lived at the same location. You do not want to be confused with someone who has tax liens, bankruptcies, or other issues that could stall or totally derail the sale.

## How to Take Title?

As part of the escrow process, you will also be asked how you want to take title, or how title should be vested. There are several different ways to hold title to real property, and they vary from state to state. I suggest that, if you have any questions, you consult an attorney and/or an accountant, as the manner in which you hold title impacts what happens to the property in the event one of the owners passes away. I'm not an attorney and can not advise you, but here is a guide to help you understand the options here in California.

Real property in California can be owned by one person, *sole ownership*, or more than one, *co-ownership*. Here are the most common ways in which title is held:

## Sole Ownership

1. **A Single Man or Woman.** A man or woman who is not legally married.

2. **An Unmarried Man or Woman.** A man or woman who was married but is now divorced or widowed.

3. **A Married Man/Woman as His/Her Sole and Separate Property.** In order for a married person to take title as sole owner, the spouse must relinquish all rights, title, and interest to the property. This is usually done with a quitclaim deed that is recorded concurrently with the property deed.

## Co-Ownership

1. **Community Property.** This is for a married couple who equally share title and right to control, manage, and sell their half. Either may will their share of the property to someone other than their spouse, but that transfer will be subject to administration of the estate. If they do not have a will or leave it specifically for their spouse, it passes to the spouse without probate.

2. **Joint Tenancy.** In a joint tenancy, two or more people hold title in equal shares. The chief characteristic of a joint tenancy is right of survivorship. When one of the joint tenants passes away, their share passes directly to the remaining owners and is not subject to probate. In a joint tenancy, an owner may not will their share to anyone inside or outside the joint tenancy.

3. **Tenancy in Common.** Under tenancy in common, two or more co-owners own undivided interests; but

unlike joint tenancy, their interests in the property are not necessarily equal in quantity or duration, and may arise at different times. There is no right of survivorship, and, at death, the percent of ownership passes to the deceased's heirs.

4. **Living Trust.** A living trust is a popular way to hold title because when someone passes away, the public probate process is avoided. Like a will, a living trust outlines the details of who will inherit the property. Stocks and other items of value may also be included in the trust.

5. **Community Property with Rights of Survivorship.** This is an option for a married couple that combines the features of holding title as community property with the benefits of the rights of survivorship. At the death of one spouse, their interest in the property will automatically pass to the other.

## More about the Escrow Process

The escrow officer will also review the Preliminary Title Report that is issued prior to the actual title insurance policy, making sure there are no potential "red flags," such as tax or mechanics liens, encroachments, easements, local violations, or judgments that have to be cleared or disclosed in order to transfer clear title to the buyers. Owner's title insurance will not be issued until title to the property can be transferred without defect. (More about title insurance in the following chapter.)

If you are financing the purchase, your escrow officer will also be responsible for coordinating with your lender to meet their closing instructions, including ordering payoff demands for any existing loans and liens, and making sure that new hazard insurance and lender's title insurance policies are in place prior to closing. He or she will also coordinate with you the signing of the new loan documents before a notary, the deposit of the balance of your down payment, and the wire transfer from the lender with the funds for the new loan.

## Understanding Prorations

One of the most important jobs of the escrow officer, and one of the most confusing to buyers and sellers, is balancing the money according to the day of closing. In California, for instance, if a seller has not paid the first installment of their property taxes (which become delinquent on December 10th), and the property is scheduled to close on December 8th, a buyer might worry about getting stuck with paying that whole first installment tax payment. That is not the case. The escrow officer is responsible for prorating taxes, and if applicable, HOA fees to the day of closing. Thus, in the above example, the seller would be responsible for the property taxes from July 1-December 8, and the buyer would be responsible for December 9–10 as well as the second installment, which is due February 1st and delinquent April 10th.

Mortgage interest is also prorated, which again can be confusing. Unlike rent that is paid in advance of each month, mortgage interest is paid in arrears. Thus, when you pay your mortgage on the first of the month, you are actually paying for the use of that money (the interest) during the previous month. At closing, you will pre-pay interest from the date of closing to the first of the next month. So, if you close escrow on December 8th, you will pre-pay interest from the 8th until December 31st, but you won't have a mortgage payment due until February 1st, at which time you'll be paying interest for

January. You will receive an estimated settlement statement during the escrow process, including the Closing Disclosure (CD), at least three days before closing. This 3-day window gives you time to compare your original estimated settlement statement provided by your lender and the final terms.

## Escrow or Impound Account

There is another use for the term "escrow" that often confuses first-time buyers. When financing a home purchase, or when refinancing, a lender will sometimes set up an "escrow" or "impound" account for the borrower. Every month when the borrower pays their mortgage, the lender is also collecting a percentage of the annual hazard insurance premium and property taxes. These funds are deposited into the borrower's escrow or impound account held by the lender. When property taxes and the insurance premium are due, those bills are paid by the lender directly, not the borrower. The advantage to this is that you don't need to worry about saving money for those bills. But, on the flip side, you are not able to put that money to work in any way while it is sitting in the lender's account. With that said, an escrow or impound account is recommended for first-time buyers.

## Close of Escrow

So, when does escrow close? Real estate closings in California rarely involve everyone sitting at a table and signing papers, then handing over keys. Typically, once the lender has funded the loan—or all buyer funds are deposited in an all-cash transaction—the title company will record the deed at the County Recorder's Office and provide confirmation of recording to the escrow officer, who will then notify both the buyer and seller. Recording confirms that title to the property has successfully passed to the buyer and arrangements are made to deliver the keys. This signals escrow has officially closed. The final job of the escrow officer at this point is to perform a closing audit on the escrow account and disburse the proceeds to the seller; pay any demands or invoices, such as termite work or warranties; pay commissions to brokers; and mail a check to the buyer if there was an overage in the estimated amount of their costs. The escrow officer then issues a certified closing statement (or HUD1, as the form is called), showing the final accounting of all funds.

If all of this still sounds a bit overwhelming, rest assured you can (and should) ask questions about any aspect of the escrow process that seems confusing. Escrow is the most important part of the sales process, and your agent and escrow officer are there to make sure you are comfortable every step of the way.

SAVVY SHOPPER TIPS: If your real estate agent has a favorite escrow officer, it is likely because they provide great service. Trust your real estate agent's recommendation. If some of the fees appear high, ask for a reduction or at least an explanation. If this is your first purchase, talk to a lawyer about how to take title. If you are financing your purchase, close later in the month to reduce the amount of pre-paid interest you'll pay. Carefully review the estimated settlement statement and Closing Disclosure, and ask questions about any line items you don't understand.

# CHAPTER 13
## THE TRUTH ABOUT TITLE INSURANCE

*A title officer recently shared a story with me about a couple who were getting ready to close escrow on their dream home in one of San Diego's nicest communities. They were especially excited about the lavish outdoor entertainment area that included a pool, spa, kitchen, and bar. The current owners had just finished the project a couple of days before they learned the husband was being transferred out of state. The couple purchasing the property were paying cash, so they weren't required to purchase title insurance for a lender, and they didn't really see the need for the added expense. They closed escrow and happily moved into their new home.*

*They soon learned that the previous owners had not finished paying the contractor for the entertainment area and pool, and the contractor had filed a mechanics lien against the property. As title had transferred without the lien being paid, the new owners were now responsible for paying the $40,000 balance! This would have been discovered in a title search had the buyers purchased title insurance. Tough way to learn a lesson!*

Accoording to Fidelity National Title Company, "title problems are discovered in more than one-third of residential real estate transactions."[1] Some common title problems, or "defects" as they are known, range from existing liens, judgments, and unpaid mortgages to errors in recorded names, addresses, and legal descriptions.[2] A title defect left unresolved can lead to legal battles down the road and even loss of property.

## What It Is

Title insurance, unlike all other types of insurance, insures against what has happened *prior* to the policy being issued, as opposed to after issuance. This means the owner and lender are insured that the title to the property is free of defects, and they are protected against future claims. There are two separate policies issued: one for the new owner, and if there is a new loan, one for the lender protecting the lender's interest in the property. Title insurance is a one-time purchase paid through escrow that remains in effect so long as you own the home, and in the case of the lender, so long as they hold a mortgage on the property. The price of title insurance is based on the sales price of the property and any upgrades added to the policy.

Over the course of time, there may be many entities that have some sort of rights in any given property; owners, heirs, and even government agencies or utility companies. In recent times in the US, changes to title have typically been recorded,

---

1. Fidelity National Title, *California Buyer & Seller Guide to Title & Escrow* (Fidelity National Title, 2012), accessed June 2018, http://zabemortgage.com/wp-content/uploads/2016/04/ZABE_Fidelity_EscrowBuyerSellerGuide.pdf.
2. Ibid.

which helps maintain the "chain of title" and makes clear the rights of all parties as they pertain to a particular property. However, even when recorded, there can be hidden risks, such as forgery, incapacity of signers, impersonation, and unknown errors. Title insurance helps protect you against these unknown and often hidden issues.

## How It Works

When the listing agent opens escrow, the escrow officer will open a title order with the selected title insurance company. Generally, the title company is selected by the seller, often based on the recommendation of the listing agent. The title order is then passed to a department within the title company that is responsible for research. This is a complicated process, as many records are not digitized and often require manual investigation. In the course of the research, the chain of title will be examined, looking to make sure each time title has passed from one person to another there are no gaps, errors, or any questionable succession. All deeds and records are collected, including a plat map showing the property in relationship to surrounding parcels. A search is also done by a local tax service to verify the status of current property taxes and any liens that may have been filed against the property.

Once all of this information is gathered, a title officer reviews the data and issues a Preliminary Title Report, which is shared with the buyers, sellers, escrow officer, agents, and the new lender. This report is issued prior to issuance of an actual title policy and will list any matters that may be exceptions to the coverage. For instance, an existing deed of trust, items recorded in the Declaration of Covenants, Codes, and Restrictions (CC&Rs), or a judgment may be listed as exceptions. Some exceptions, such as an existing deed of trust or judgment, must be removed prior to title passing and issuance of a new title policy, while other items, such as utility easements or CC&Rs, pass along with the property. This is why it's important for all parties to carefully examine the Preliminary Title Report.

The title officer will also examine the buyer's and seller's Statement of Information in order to verify the legitimacy of their identities. Once the necessary exceptions have been removed and the identities verified, and once the purchase funds have been wired to escrow by the buyer and lender, the new title and, if applicable, new deed of trust, will be recorded. After recording, the title officer will write the policy and release it to the new owner and lender.

## Policy Types

There are two basic types of title insurance policies issued in California: CLTA and ALTA. The CLTA policy is issued by the California Land Title Association. This is considered a standard policy that protects against financial loss by fraud and forgery and recorded claims or unpaid taxes from a former owner. The ALTA policy is issued by the American Land Title Association and offers additional protections against unrecorded matters, such as encroachments and boundary disputes, among other items. Many title companies also offer an upgraded policy that goes beyond both the CLTA and ALTA policies in terms of expanded protection. It's a good idea to review these policies with your title officer to see which level of coverage you really need.

SAVVY SHOPPER TIPS: Always purchase title insurance, even if paying cash. Investigate the types of policies offered. Lenders generally require an ALTA policy because of the extended coverage. Before purchasing an upgraded ALTA policy, review carefully to see if you really need the additional coverage. Always read your Preliminary Title Report carefully and ask questions about any exceptions you were not aware of, such as easements or encroachments.

# CHAPTER 14
## HOME INSPECTION AND REPAIRS
## WHAT SHOULD A BUYER EXPECT?

*I have a very good client who I've helped buy five investment properties over the years. He is a smart guy and now owns about 19 properties. On every property, however, he has ignored my repeated suggestion that he get a home inspection, insisting he knows what to look for and an inspection is a waste of money for him. He may, however, change his mind next time around, as he just learned the hard (and expensive) way that a home inspection really can save you money.*

*His latest purchase was a condo built in 1982. When doing his walk-through, he turned on the heater and felt warm air coming out of the ceiling vent. He then switched it to A/C and again put his hand near the vent. After a few seconds, the air coming out seemed to be cooler, so he was satisfied that the system worked to both heat and cool the home.*

*After closing escrow, he did some painting and replaced the living room carpet, getting the unit ready to rent out. One particularly warm day, one of the contractors working on the property turned on the A/C, but even after running it for 15 minutes, the air blowing into the room was barely cool. The A/C was not working.*

*My client called an HVAC repair person, who determined that the A/C unit was the original one that had been installed back in 1982, and it simply wasn't worth repairing. On the same visit, he inspected the forced air heater and determined that it too was on its last legs and should be replaced. $6000 later, my client was singing the blues.*

*A home inspection would have revealed both of these problems, and even if my client still wanted to go through with the purchase, he could have asked the seller to replace the A/C and heater, or requested a price reduction.*

W e've all heard the expression "*caveat emptor,*" meaning "let the buyer beware." And nowhere is that more true than in the purchase of a home. Whether purchasing a brand new home in the suburbs, a downtown high-rise condo, or a 100-year-old lake side cottage, a home inspection by a trained professional will not only provide you with a clear picture of the property's condition, but it could also save you thousands of dollars.

## What Is a Home Inspection?

A home inspection is a detailed examination of the interior of a residence and the immediate exterior area that identifies any health or safety concerns as well as any system or structural problems that might require repair or replacement. The report is usually broken down into categories, such as electrical, plumbing, roofing, HVAC, foundation, grading, etc. Within each category, the items inspected are identified and commented on by the inspector. So, for instance, when examining a water heater, the inspector may note that it is only a year old and functioning properly, but he might also note that it is incorrectly braced according to California law. He would then make the recommendation in his report that the earthquake bracing be corrected.

In a slow-moving market where there is little competition, a buyer might opt to pay for a home inspection *prior* to writing an offer. However, in a competitive market where buyers are writing multiple offers and time is of the essence, home inspections are ordered after an offer is accepted and escrow is opened. Unless otherwise noted in the Residential Purchase Agreement, in California, the time period for completion of all inspections is 17 days from date of acceptance.

Often, homes are advertised and sold "as-is," indicating the seller is not willing to make repairs. A home inspection is still recommended, as an inspection might reveal costly repairs that could alter your decision to purchase or perhaps renegotiate the price.

It should be noted most home inspectors are generalists, and they often suggest further evaluation by a licensed contractor in a specialized area. Most home inspectors do not climb up on your roof to inspect every valley, nor do they test wells or attempt to explain cracked walls. Their job is to report any anomaly that might, in the worst case, be a symptom of a larger problem, such as water stains in the attic or doors that don't close properly.

The length of time required to complete the inspection will vary according to the type of home, the size, and the age. These factors will also help determine the price. A 20- to 30-year-old, 2,000 square foot home with three bedrooms, two baths will probably take about 2.5–3 hours to inspect.

Very large homes may even require two inspectors, or a much longer time, and condo inspections are generally completed in a shorter inspection period. If ordering a home inspection as a buyer, it is recommended that you be present, along with your agent, so that the most important findings can be discussed with the inspector. It is also somewhat easier if the seller is not present and all rooms are accessible.

## How to Choose a Home Inspector

Many home inspectors come from some type of background in the trades, or are licensed contractors. It is also desirable that they have specific training from an accredited inspection training program and are members of one of the professional inspection organizations. In some states, licensing may be required, so it is always a good idea to ask about an inspector's credentials before your hire them.

Besides credentials and training, there are other important considerations, including the type of technologies they use. One of the most useful is an infrared thermal imaging camera. This allows the inspector to point the camera at a wall or appliance and check moisture and heat levels. This may reveal a small hidden pipe leak in a wall or a circuit breaker that is overheating; problems not visible to the naked eye, but real potential concerns. Many inspectors today are also taking advantage of drone technology or giant selfie sticks to get a more thorough view of the roof.

It is also a good idea to inquire about the format of the report itself. For any item an inspector comments on, it is useful if there is an accompanying photo included in the report that specifically identifies the problem. Without a photo, you may be scratching your head a month from now asking, "Which pipe is he referring to?" Handwritten reports are becoming a thing of the past. A well-organized report created with a software program and saved as a PDF file is the new industry standard. This is a report that is legible and can be easily saved for future reference, or sent to the listing agent or a contractor for comments or quotes.

If you're unsure about where to begin your search for an inspector, ask your real estate agent for one or more recommendations. If they've been in the business for any time at all, they have probably located a local inspector they trust to do a thorough job.

## *What Does the Seller Have to Repair?*

Unless you are purchasing a brand new home with a builder's warranty, the answer is "not much." In California, the seller is required to have the water heater properly braced and smoke and CO detectors installed in specific locations throughout the home. If you are purchasing with a VA or FHA loan, your lender may require that some items be in working order prior to close of escrow. That being said, it isn't always the responsibility of the seller to fix those items, and repairs may be a matter of negotiation.

One thing to keep in mind when you first see the inspection report is that no home is perfect, especially a resale home, and over time the number of flaws generally increases. The inspection report is not a laundry list to hand to the seller with a request to repair everything. Rather, it is a reference guide that provides a broad picture of the condition of the home and helps you prioritize repairs and improvements. The report will make several distinctions for each item inspected, indicating whether the item is dysfunctional versus deficient and whether or not it should be replaced or repaired.

The process of determining what to ask the seller to repair should start with what you are paying for the home and how many repairs are necessary. If you are paying top dollar, you are in a better position to expect the seller to make repairs or to provide a credit to cover the costs of repairs. On the other hand, if you got a steal of a deal on the home, or purchased a short sale or REO, it is unlikely repairs will be made or a credit provided.

Another thing to consider is whether or not you had knowledge of the needed repair prior to writing your offer. If it is obvious to even an untrained eye the roof needs to be replaced, that should have been taken into account when writing your offer, and it is unlikely the seller will cover that cost. However, if as a result of the home inspection you discover that the entire HVAC system is inoperable, that is likely not something you knew prior to writing an offer. That would be an expensive repair and one you might ask the seller to make, or provide as a credit.

Repairs are negotiable, but when asking for seller repairs or credits, it is in everyone's best interests to be reasonable. Ask for the big-ticket repairs if appropriate, and just figure that you'll take care of the smaller items, like a broken outlet cover or a torn window screen.

A home inspection is always important, even for an experienced investor. Not everything is immediately apparent on a walk-through. Think of it this way: A home inspection is rather like being able to fast-forward in a marriage by five years and learn all about your spouse *before* the wedding day! Certainly not an opportunity to be missed.

SAVVY SHOPPER TIPS: Always get a home inspection, as the benefits far outweigh the cost. Don't panic when you see the report. It is the job of the inspector to note all anomalies and no home is perfect. Discuss the report with your agent and determine which repairs are the most important to address. Do not ask for everything to be fixed unless you're purchasing a brand new home.

# CHAPTER 15
## UH-OH! A WORD ABOUT
## REAL ESTATE DISCLOSURES

*Several years ago, I was contacted by a couple who wanted to sell their home ASAP, despite the fact they had only lived in it for a few months. They explained that, after closing escrow on a Friday, they were awakened the next morning by the very loud whirring of 100+ motorcycles, and it was non-stop until 6 p.m. It turns out that down in a canyon about a quarter mile from their home is a dirt motorcycle track that is only open on the weekends. When house hunting, they had only viewed the home on weekdays, and as the track is not visible or accessible from the street where their house is located, they had no idea it even existed.*

*They were devastated! Their decision to buy in that particular community was because it was out in the country and quiet! Later when speaking to the neighbors, they also learned that the reason they were able to purchase the home at such a low price was that home values had dropped over the last few years, as the track had become more and more popular and the noise level grew.*

> *Their disappointment quickly turned to anger. Why hadn't the previous owners disclosed information about the track and the noise? Why hadn't their agent warned them? She worked in that community and certainly knew about the noise issue.*
>
> *While there is a certain level of responsibility that falls on the buyer, in this situation, the seller and their agent were clearly at fault for not disclosing the noise nuisance. We managed to get their house sold, with full disclosure about the noise, but they sold at a loss. They sued the sellers and the agent, and to the best of my knowledge, they're still battling. So, not only did they lose money on the purchase and sale, but they've also racked up thousands in legal fees. As I always tell my sellers, disclose, disclose, disclose!*

## Two Basic Categories of Real Estate Disclosures

The number of disclosures now required by law has increased over time as a result of legal actions, often taken by buyers against sellers who failed to disclose pertinent information about the property, as illustrated in my story above. A disclosure pertaining to a specific property prepared by the seller who has knowledge of the property is the first category of disclosures. This would also include disclosures about whether there is an HOA, or any special fees associated with owning the property. Although the laws vary, every state now requires sellers to provide some sort of disclosure about their knowledge of the property, including any potential safety hazards or conditions that could increase the expense of ownership or reduce the value of the property.

The second category of disclosures are those referencing existing conditions that may be inside or outside the home and unknown to the seller, such as the home being in a flood zone or fire danger zone. Some of these disclosures are prepared by companies who analyze the location of a specific property in relation to hazards, such as earthquake zones or airports. This information is compiled into a Natural Hazard Disclosure (NHD) Report, which is typically ordered by the seller's agent, paid for by the seller, and delivered to the buyer. Along with the NHD, several other informational booklets may be delivered to the buyer, covering topics such as earthquake safety, environmental hazards in the home, and energy conservation. These are typically issued by the state or local authorities as a means of educating homeowners about potential health and safety concerns.

## California Real Estate Disclosures

As noted above, it is the responsibility of the seller to pass along all pertinent information about a property to the buyer, including any reports or inspections. Failure to disclose could result in fines or liability for the seller for any resulting damages. In California, there are many disclosures and some are specific to particular situations, such as a short sale or purchasing a foreclosure.

In the following list, I've put together a brief description of the most common disclosures used in the sale of a 1- to 4-unit residential property. These disclosures are offered by the California Association of REALTORS and made available to agents licensed in the state. Other forms may be legally acceptable, but these are the forms most commonly used. They are often referred to by their initials, which I've included next to the names.

- **Agency Disclosures** (AD)—Clearly identifies the agents and brokers who are representing the buyer and the seller.

- **Agent Visual Inspection Disclosure** (AVID)—Agents visually inspect the property and make note of specific issues or attributes that are easily identified, such as a hole in a wall or a broken window. They are not responsible for doing a home inspection or testing appliances.

- **Transfer Disclosure Statement** (TDS)—A comprehensive statement regarding the condition of the property. This is completed by the seller unless the seller has never lived in the property; in which case, they are exempt from completing.

- **Seller Property Questionnaire** (SPQ)—Used in addition to the TDS or when a TDS is not required. The SPQ provides the buyer with additional information about known material facts regarding the property.

- **Statewide Buyer and Seller Advisory** (SBSA)—A comprehensive list of all conditions that both buyers and sellers should consider investigating in the course of the transaction.

- **Buyer's Inspection Advisory** (BIA)—A list of conditions the buyer is advised to investigate as part of their due diligence during the inspection period.

- **Market Condition Advisory** (MCA)—Advises both buyers and sellers that no guarantees are made regarding the future value of the property, as real estate markets can change.

- **Megan's Law Database Disclosure** (DBD)—Advises buyers and sellers that through a website maintained by the Department of Justice they may obtain information about the address or residence community and zip code of registered sex offenders.

## What to Look for in Reading Real Estate Disclosures

Disclosures should always be read in their entirety. These are legal documents and, by signing, you are stating that you have read and understood everything that is disclosed in a particular document. If you don't understand, or need clarification on a certain item, please discuss this with your agent before signing. With that said, here are a few key items you'll want to make sure you've reviewed thoroughly:

- In the NHD report, make sure to note if you are in a special flood zone, as this may mean that you will need flood insurance. Likewise, if you are in a fire danger zone, it might be more difficult or costly to obtain your homeowner's insurance. And if you are in an earthquake hazard zone, earthquake insurance may be something to consider. It is also important to notice if you are in an airport flight path or in an area with commercial/ industrial zoning, as these influences may cause noise or other disturbances.

- On the SPQ and TDS, or on any disclosure form completed by the sellers, if any of the "yes" boxes are checked, there needs to be an explanation written directly below that block of questions or noted on an attached sheet if necessary. Depending on the situation, you may want to request receipts, inspection reports, or invoices to see exactly how repairs, if applicable, were made.

## *What to Do with a Negative Discovery*

It is sometimes the case in the course of reviewing disclosures that you'll discover a condition or issue you were unaware of at the time you wrote your offer. So, for instance, in the story I mentioned at the top of the chapter, if the proximity of the motorcycle track had been disclosed, the buyers would have had the opportunity to pull out of the deal, provided this was within their contingency period, or they might have negotiated a lower price. In another example, let's say the seller discloses that the insulation around some of the duct work contains asbestos. It is unlikely the buyer would know this at the time of writing an offer, and while undisturbed asbestos may not be an immediate health concern, it would be in the future should the duct work need repair or replacement. Looking ahead to that possibility may prompt the buyer to ask for a price reduction to help cover the future cost of removing the asbestos-containing materials.

Another situation I've observed is when a homeowner discloses a past problem, such as a roof leak, but then notes he or she fixed it themselves. Many home repairs can be accomplished by the homeowner, but in a situation like this, you may want to request that the homeowner provide an inspection of the repairs by a licensed professional, just to make sure the problem was indeed fixed and the work was done to code.

While the seller is responsible for providing complete disclosure about all known facts about a property, the buyer bears the responsibility of making sure they are satisfied with all explanations and that they thoroughly understand the implications of all items disclosed. The best time to ask questions is before you close escrow and purchase a potential problem.

SAVVY SHOPPER TIPS: Read through all disclosures carefully before signing. These are legal documents. If you have any questions about a condition on the property or any item disclosed, your inspection contingency period is the time to request a thorough explanation. If problems are disclosed, it may be an opportunity to renegotiate the price, or get out of the deal entirely.

# CHAPTER 16
## WHEN THE APPRAISAL BRINGS A SURPRISE

As part of the loan-approval process, your lender will hire a licensed appraiser to view your future home, research the neighborhood, check comparable listings and sales, and assign a value to the home. The lender, of course, wants to make sure the amount they are lending would be recouped if you, the borrower, defaults and they have to foreclose. But what happens when the appraisal packs an unexpected blow to your deal? That's exactly what happened to my clients Mark and Rhonda. Let's take a look at their story.

*Mark and Rhonda fell in love with a family-perfect, single-story home in the North County area of San Diego. It had everything they were looking for; 4 bedrooms, 2 baths and a large lot full of native oak trees in a quiet area with other well-maintained custom homes. The only problem was the price. At $643,000, it seemed greatly overpriced when I showed them the comps, which perhaps explained why it had been on the market so long.*

*My clients wrote a significantly lower offer at $612,000, which was countered at $635,000. According to the listing agent, the sellers could not afford* *to budge a dollar below that number, as they had overextended themselves in 2005 with a second mortgage. Even at $635,000, the sellers would have to bring money to the table to close. They had investigated the possibility of a short sale but did not qualify, so this was their only hope.*

*Looking at the comps, I was very nervous about getting an appraised value of $635,000, and sure enough, the appraisal came in at $625,000—$10,000 off. The listing agent and I tried to challenge the value, but there simply weren't the comps to support it. As the sellers couldn't come down in price (since they needed to pay off two mortgages), the only options available to my buyers were to pay the extra $10,000 out of pocket or walk away. Tough decision. If it had been a lesser amount, maybe $5,000 or less, they would have paid it and considered it a premium to get the house they so dearly wanted. But at $10,000 out of pocket, it just didn't make financial sense to overpay so much, so they walked away.*

## Appraisal Types

First, it's important to understand that not all appraisals look at exactly the same thing. The type of appraisal performed will vary according to the type of loan you are getting. Thus, a VA or FHA appraisal will differ from a conventional appraisal in terms of what is inspected, the types of forms that are used, and the qualifications of the appraiser. While the value should be close regardless of the type of appraisal that's performed, there are some important differences to understand.

A conventional appraisal is based on establishing the actual value of the home, generally using the comparable sales method. The appraiser researches comparable active and sold listings that are geographically and characteristically as close as possible to your home. Value is then added or subtracted from each property for items—such as a forest view versus a truck terminal view, or an updated home versus a home showing deferred maintenance—ultimately arriving at a fair market value.

On the other hand, VA and FHA appraisals not only focus on establishing market value according to comparable sales, they also inspect the home according to certain property condition criteria. As both of these types of loans are government backed, both agencies want to make sure the homes are safe, sanitary, and structurally sound. So, when performing a VA or FHA appraisal, the appraiser will note things about the home that do not meet the VA Minimum Property Requirements or FHA criteria, such as obvious termite damage, lack of floor coverings, leaking plumbing, or no home heating. These items will be called out in the report and must be fixed and re-inspected prior to the lender funding the VA or FHA loan. This is why homes that are being sold "as-is" are difficult to purchase with a VA or FHA loan.

## Subject to Repair

Let's say you've just received your FHA appraisal back from your lender, and, unfortunately, the appraiser has called out several items that need repair. For example, if the necessary repairs include tenting the home for termites, fixing some cracked windows, and tightening the banister, the repairs could easily run close to $4000! The home's value meets the sales price, but the appraised value is "subject to" the repairs being completed. What to do now?

You basically have three options if you want to move forward with the purchase and you can't do a conventional loan: 1) Ask the seller to pay out of pocket to fix the repair items; 2) Ask the seller to lower the sales price or provide a credit at closing, and you agree to complete the repairs; or 3) Find a contractor to do the repairs who's willing to be paid out of escrow at closing. The first choice is the simplest, while the second choice can be a bit problematic and risky. As you remember, repairs must be made before the lender will agree to fund the loan. This means that you, the buyer, could be spending thousands of dollars on repairs on a home you don't yet own! If all other contingencies are removed and the loan is otherwise fully approved, it is probably okay, but you should also be aware of any worker liability issues and who would be responsible. Also, if this were a VA loan, there may be repairs the buyer is not allowed to pay. This varies by state, so it is a good idea to know in advance of obtaining a VA loan. And while finding a contractor willing to be paid out of escrow is certainly an option, they will usually ask for a credit card for security in case escrow fails to close.

If you're purchasing a short sale or REO, it is highly unlikely the short-sale lender or bank will pay for any repairs (see Chapter 8), so you're probably on your own in terms of making any necessary repairs. If you have already completed your home inspection, as mentioned in Chapter 14, you should already be aware of many of these issues, as a home inspection is always more thorough than an appraisal. So, by the time you get to the appraisal, you will have hopefully figured out a way to resolve any repair issues.

## *Value Too Low*

In a market with low inventory, we often see prices driven up by competitive bidding. However, just because you're willing to pay more to purchase a particular property, it doesn't mean that an appraiser will value the home as highly as you do. A lower valuation means that the bank is not going to lend you as much money. For instance, if you're purchasing a $510,000 home with a 20% down payment, you'll need a loan of $408,000. If the appraisal comes in at $501,000, the bank will only lend you $400,800, which means you are $7,200 short to make the deal work at $510,000.

Low appraised value can happen in a market where there are not many current sales, so the sold prices for comparable properties might reflect a fair market value from several months ago. The fact that you are willing to pay a higher price due to competition still makes it difficult to assign a higher value if there are no comps to support it.

So what can you do? Start with having your agent challenge the appraisal. They can do this by hopefully finding comps that better support the sales price and submitting them through your lender to the appraiser. If your comps are strong, there's a chance the appraiser will consider a price adjustment.

But don't count on it. It's more likely they will stick to their original valuation; in which case, here are your choices: 1) Accept the lower valuation and pay the difference out of pocket; 2) Ask the seller to carry back a small second mortgage; or 3) Ask the seller to reduce the price. Obviously, asking the seller to reduce the price is your most favorable solution, but if it is a hot property with multiple offers, and if the appraised price isn't ridiculously lower, there's a good chance the seller will expect the buyer to make up the difference out of pocket. It should also be noted that if the seller takes back a small second mortgage, the monthly payment on that lien will count against your debt-to-income ratio, which may impact your ability to qualify for the first mortgage.

One note here about the VA/FHA Amendatory Clause: If you are getting a VA or FHA loan, this document ensures that you don't have to go through with the purchase if the appraised value is less than the contract sales price, basically letting you off the hook without losing your earnest money deposit. But even if you're using conventional financing, it is likely you will not have to complete the purchase if the appraised value is low, as most contracts have a provision that makes the purchase contingent upon the appraisal.

SAVVY SHOPPER TIPS: If you're financing your purchase, make sure the purchase offer reads that the sale is contingent upon the property appraising at sales price or higher. Do not expect to use FHA or VA financing on a home that obviously needs major repairs—at minimum, it must be habitable. Don't be afraid to challenge a low appraisal if your real estate agent thinks they can make a case for a higher valuation. A bidding war or higher-than-asking-price offer may be a good strategy on a financed deal if you really love the home. This may help get your offer accepted, and you do have options if the appraisal comes in lower than contract price. Paying a reasonable out-of-pocket premium to get the house you want may be worth it, especially if you plan on owning the home for a number of years, during which time the home will hopefully appreciate.

# CHAPTER 17
## WHAT INSURANCE DO YOU REALLY
## NEED WHEN PURCHASING A HOME?

B uying a home is likely the single largest purchase you will make, and it's therefore important to protect your investment by insuring it against loss. But what type of insurance do you need, and how do you find a good, yet affordable, policy? In this chapter, I take you through the various types of insurance and answer the most common questions I hear from home buyers.

## *Homeowner's Insurance*

The primary type of insurance you will need is homeowner's or hazard insurance. This type of insurance comes in several forms, depending on the type of property and the perils covered. Thus, the insurance needed for a condo or townhome will differ from the policy needed for a single-family detached home. A homeowner's policy covers various protections for losses to the property itself, personal property, and liability for accidents that might occur on the property. When purchasing a condo, the HOA generally has a master policy that covers the actual structure of your home, but it does not cover anything on the interior, such as cabinets or flooring, or personal property. Those items will need to be covered in a separate homeowner's policy that you, as the buyer, purchase.

The cost of your insurance will be based on a number of factors, including the cost to rebuild the house in case of destruction (replacement cost), the location of the property, the amount of coverage and deductibles, and factors such as having a security or fire sprinkler system, which might qualify for a discount. For instance, a home that is situated on the edge of a brush-filled canyon will likely pay a higher premium than a home that does not abut open space, as the risk of fire is greater.

When selecting a policy, it is important to understand exactly what is covered, and what is not covered. The most common type of policy will include perils—such as fire, lightning, burst pipes, vandalism, civil riot, theft, and falling objects, to name a few—but it does not cover against flood or earthquakes. Personal property will also be covered up to a certain amount, usually 50% of total coverage. But it is important to note there are limits on jewelry, artwork, cameras, firearms, stamp collections, and other valuables. With that said, I'd like to share a story.

*Several years ago, one of my REALTOR friends told me a story about her friend Diane. Diane and her husband attended a very dressy New Year's Eve party to which she wore what had been her mother's diamond necklace. The necklace contained one beautiful 1.2 carat diamond and two smaller .5 carat diamonds. The necklace had been appraised at $15,000 at the time Diane inherited it from her mother in 2010.*

*Normally, Diane kept the necklace locked away in the safe in their home, but she was tired when they got home from the party and slipped it into the top drawer of her dresser, figuring that she would store it properly in the morning.*

*New Year's Day brought a headache and a reminder from her husband they were expected at a friend's house on the other side of town for an afternoon of football and food. Diane pulled herself together and left with her husband for another round of partying with friends, totally forgetting about locking away the necklace.*

*The couple returned later that evening to discover that, in their haste to leave earlier, they had neglected to set the alarm and someone had broken into their house from the rear entrance. The home was torn apart and cameras, computers, and TVs were gone, as were several expensive handbags...and the diamond necklace.*

*Diane was devastated. The necklace meant so much to her! But she was even more upset when she learned that their homeowner's policy only covered up to $1,500 on jewelry loss.*

As this story illustrates, if you have valuables that exceed the personal property limits of your insurance, they should be insured separately on what is known as a *rider*. The amount you will pay extra to insure individual items will depend on their value as appraised by a qualified specialist. Your insurance agent will let you know the requirements for assigning value, depending on whether the insured items are jewelry, artwork, or other valuables.

If you are purchasing the home with a loan, the lender will require they be named as loss payee on the policy and will generally require the first year's premium to be paid upfront through escrow. If you are establishing an impound account to pay your taxes and insurance with your mortgage payment, the lender will additionally require a deposit of 2 to 3 months' insurance payments to establish the account.

## Shopping for Homeowner's Insurance

One of the first places to begin shopping for homeowner's insurance is with the company that carries your automobile policy, as most large companies will provide a multiple-policy discount. These days, it is relatively easy to get several quotes, as you can search and complete requests for quotes online. Before you sit down at your computer, however, make sure you are prepared with information about the home you are purchasing, including square footage, age, type and age of roof, location of the nearest fire hydrant, and any special preventative features, such as fire sprinklers or a security system. It is also important to know if your home falls within a flood zone, as this might mean you will need additional flood insurance as well.

When evaluating quotes, price is not the only consideration. It is a good idea to inquire about the company's rating, as this reflects their financial strength. Ratings go from A+++, which is superior, down to a D-, which is poor. Obviously, if you have a claim, you want to make sure the company is financially strong enough to pay your claim, so a higher rating is preferable. You may also want to search for comments from customers about their claims experience, especially how long it took for claims to be processed and payments received. Additionally, if you will not be paying through an impound account, be sure to inquire as to what type of payments are available, as some companies do not offer monthly payments and require you to pay in one annual or two semi-annual payments.

## Flood Insurance

You may also want to consider flood insurance offered through the National Flood Insurance Program (NFIP), which is run by the Federal Emergency Management Agency (FEMA). As noted earlier, water damage from a burst pipe is covered in your homeowner's insurance, but flooding from storms and hurricanes or dam inundation is not. Flood insurance is based on the replacement cost for your home's structure and actual cash value for personal property.

During the inspection period of your purchase transaction, you will receive many disclosures, including a Natural Hazard Disclosure Report, as noted in Chapter 15. This report will reveal whether or not you are in a flood zone. It should be noted, however, that even if the property you are buying is outside a zone on a flood map, over 20% of flood insurance claims are filed in areas of low to moderate flood risk.

Flood insurance policies are written by over 100 insurance companies who participate in the NFIP, so getting a quote is easy. It should be noted that after a policy is written and paid for, there is a 30-day waiting period before it goes into effect. In case of a flood, those who are uninsured may be eligible for low-rate loans if the area is declared a Presidential disaster area. The disadvantage, of course, is that loans must be repaid, whereas with insurance you are simply paid according to your claim. More information is available at FEMA: *www.floodsmart.gov*.

## Earthquake Insurance

The thing that makes earthquakes so scary is they are pretty much unpredictable. Although science has made great strides in the last 20 years in terms of identifying potential stress points that may trigger a quake, predicting an earthquake isn't like looking at a map and plotting the course of a hurricane or a swollen river. Earthquakes arrive with little to no warning, and as we have witnessed, can cause massive destruction of property.

What many people don't understand is that no matter where you live in the US, damage from an earthquake is not covered by your homeowner's insurance policy. Earthquake insurance is a separate policy, similar to flood insurance. In California, earthquake insurance is issued by the California Earthquake Authority (CEA). What might surprise you is, despite California's earthquake history, fewer than 12% of homeowners have earthquake insurance.

In the past, few people had earthquake insurance because of the high 15% deductible. With homeowner's insurance, your deductible is a flat amount, such as $2,500, but with earthquake insurance, your deductible is a percentage of your home's value. A 15% deductible on a home valued at $600,000 would be $90,000! That is a lot to spend before your insurance kicks in. Today in California, there are options for policies that have deductibles as low as 5%, and as high as 25%, which you can explore at the California Earthquake Authority: *http://www.earthquakeauthority.com*.

Should you consider earthquake insurance? The answer might depend on where your home is located. As noted earlier, during your inspection period, you will receive a Natural Hazard Disclosure Report, which, in addition to showing whether or not your home is in a flood zone, will show your proximity to earthquake faults. Depending on your home's proximity to a fault, the cost of your home, and your financial resources, earthquake insurance might be a wise choice.

SAVVY SHOPPER TIPS: Do shop around for your insurance, as there is often a difference in premiums between companies of several hundred dollars a year for the same coverage. Check the limits on what is covered for jewelry and other valuables, and insure those items on a separate schedule with a rider. Do check on proximity to flood or earthquake zones, and make sure you are adequately protected.

# CHAPTER 18
## WHEN YOU SHOULD AND SHOULDN'T PURCHASE A HOME WARRANTY

Homes operate as a complex network of systems and appliances. When everything works as it should, your home operates smoothly and you really don't think about the complicated nature of everything going on behind your walls. But when the shower won't turn off, or the furnace fails to provide heat, your world turns upside down. Not only are these failures inconvenient, they can be very costly to repair or replace.

## What Does a Home Warranty Cover?

Home warranties are not the same as homeowner's insurance, which provides coverage for fire, theft, and other hazards. *Home warranties are basically a service contract that pays for the repair or replacement of certain components within your home that fail because of malfunction and normal wear and tear.* Most basic warranties cover electrical, heating, and duct work as well as plumbing, kitchen appliances (except refrigerators), and exhaust fans for a period of one year. The cost for a basic policy is $300-$500 for a single-family home, and slightly less for a condo. For an additional $100-$250 per item, there is additional extended coverage available for A/C, pools, refrigerators, washers and dryers, and even roof leaks, among other items. Warranties for larger homes can cost up to $1,000. Warranty terms are generally one year, with some offering 13 months of coverage.

## Do I Really Need One?

Whether you should buy coverage or not depends on a few factors. For instance, if you are purchasing a brand new home, the builder will provide at least a one-year warranty for home systems and appliances, and generally ten years for structural issues. If your home comes with appliances, those will additionally have manufacturer's warranties.

On the other hand, if you are purchasing a resale home, it may be a good idea to purchase a warranty, or ask the seller to provide one as part of your negotiation. This could be especially important if you are a first-time buyer sinking all of your money into the down payment—you could end up in a precarious financial position if faced with an expensive repair in your first year of ownership. Often, your real estate agent will pay for the home warranty as a way to thank you for your business. A home warranty purchased by the seller before the house is even sold can be an attractive incentive to prospective buyers, as the warranty will transfer to them upon closing.

As with any contract, the key is to carefully read the information and be aware of exactly what is covered and what is not. For instance, roots in a sewer line are not covered, nor are appliances that were installed incorrectly. Also, be aware there will always be a service call fee of $50-$75, and you cannot use the repair company of your choice. If you have an appliance or system failure and you think it will be covered, call your home warranty company right away before calling an outside technician or trying to repair it yourself, as these actions might invalidate any claim you could otherwise make.

Before we wrap up our discussion on home warranties, I'd like to share another personal story.

*My husband and I actually had an interesting experience with a home warranty the seller had purchased for us on a home we bought back in 2001. Shortly after moving in, we had a heat wave and turned on the A/C, which had worked fine during the inspection. It ran for about an hour cooling the home, and then it stopped blowing cold air and just ran like a fan. We contacted the home warranty company, and they sent out a repair person the next day. After a thorough inspection, the repair person determined that the A/C unit was so old it really wasn't worth repairing, and our warranty company authorized the replacement of the unit. We were, of course, very happy we had that warranty!*

If you will be purchasing a warranty, or asking for one, it is wise to do some online research to explore the different warranties available; what they cover, exclusions, limitations, costs, and reviews from actual customers. Doing your homework before purchasing a home warranty could provide not only peace of mind, but also save you money and headaches down the road.

SAVVY SHOPPER TIPS: A home warranty may be advisable if you are purchasing a resale home. Ask for a warranty to be included when you write your purchase offer. If purchasing a warranty yourself, be sure to shop around and do read customer reviews. Some home warranty companies can be quick to sell you a policy but a nightmare when you go to file a claim. If the appliances are newer, it might be a waste of money to pay for an upgraded warranty that includes appliances, such as a refrigerator or washer and dryer that may already be covered by a transferable manufacturer's warranty.

# CHAPTER 19
## JUST SIGN HERE
## UNDERSTANDING YOUR LOAN
## DOCUMENTS

*When I first started in real estate back in 2005, I worked as a loan officer in what was certainly the most corrupt period for lending in our lifetime. Abuses and greed were rampant, as banks and mortgage bankers kept reducing the qualifications necessary to get a home loan. This was very evident in San Diego, where some unscrupulous mortgage brokers preyed upon our large Spanish-speaking population and talked them into signing documents they could not read, for loans they could never afford. Even English speakers were at a loss to understand the intricacies of a negative amortization loan and what that really meant in the long term. The almost non-existent qualification requirements, inflated loan amounts, and crazy terms were so unrealistic that many borrowers were doomed to foreclosure or a short sale before the ink had even dried on the loan docs. I also knew of appraisers who would willingly inflate property values, allowing homeowners to drain imaginary equity from their homes. The inevitable burst of the housing bubble threw our country into the Great Re-*

*cession and devastated the housing market. For those of us in the business, it was a very bumpy road.*

*As of this writing, it is a much safer environment for today's borrowers. We saw the tightening of lending guidelines, changes in how appraisals are ordered, and the birth of the Consumer Financial Protection Bureau. While it is always important to read what you are signing, your chances of getting a loan you don't understand are greatly reduced in today's market.*

The time is finally here—you're *really* buying a home and it's time to sign the loan documents. The notary opens a folder, and you gasp as you see a pile of papers the size of a small phone book. What the heck are you signing, and how can you possibly read through all of these pages and feel confident that you're not giving away your first-born child?

## The Documents You'll Be Signing

The good news is that if you and your lender have both done your jobs, there will be no surprises. From the very beginning of the application process, your lender is required to deliver certain documents to you within three days of receiving your application—their job is to deliver the documents, your job is to read them carefully and ask questions. The loan estimate you receive at that time shows your loan amount, interest rate, term, line-item fees, and the cash you need to close the transaction. If you originally did a pre-approval before opening escrow, the estimate will be changed based on the final sales price and terms of the purchase.

You will have another opportunity to review your loan three days prior to closing escrow, when the lender is required to provide a Closing Disclosure (CD). This disclosure is very similar to the loan estimate and will again show your loan amount, interest rate, term, line-item fees, and the cash you need to close the transaction. The CD is delivered to you and signed just before loan docs are drawn by the lender and sent to escrow. This provides you, the borrower, with one final opportunity to review the numbers before committing to the loan.

So, when you see that big stack of papers, there should be no surprises. Here are the main documents you'll be signing:

- **The Note**—The promissory note is your promise to repay the loan and the accrued interest. It will show the loan amount, term, interest rate, due date, date of first payment, where to pay, and penalties for late payment.

- **Mortgage or Deed of Trust**—Whether you sign a mortgage or a deed of trust depends on where the property is located. In California, a deed of trust is most commonly used. Both documents establish your home as collateral to protect the lender's interests in case you stop making payments. A mortgage is an agreement between the lender and the borrower. A deed of trust also includes a third-party trustee, often a title company, who acts as a representative of the lender in case of foreclosure. Another difference between the two documents is that in case of foreclosure, the trustee can expedite the sale of the property, whereas if there is a mortgage, a judicial proceeding is usually required.

- **The Deed**—This document officially transfers ownership of the property from the seller to the buyer. The deed is recorded with the County Recorder's Office, providing public evidence of the sale and the transfer of ownership.

- **HUD-1**—This is a standard real estate settlement form that is used throughout the country. It itemizes all the charges and credits associated with the transaction. You will receive a HUD-1 three days prior to closing, and then a final certified copy after escrow closes. The final HUD-1 is an important document to retain, as there are certain closing costs that are tax deductible.

Depending on the type of loan, you may also be signing an affidavit that you will be occupying the property. This is likely if you have a VA or FHA loan. If you have an adjustable-rate loan, you will also sign an additional document outlining the adjustments and terms of the loan. Another document is also signed if you are setting up an escrow account to pay your insurance and property taxes on a monthly basis along with your mortgage payment. *The most important thing to do when signing is to make certain that the loan amount, interest rate, and all other terms match what was previously disclosed.* It is also important that you bring your driver's license or passport to the signing as identification for the notary.

## What Happens After You Sign?

What happens next will vary from state to state. After signing in California, the notary will return all the paperwork to the escrow company. Once the documents are inspected for accuracy and completeness, they are returned to the lender, who will also inspect the documents. If anything is lacking or inaccurate in the lender's loan package, the underwriter may issue funding conditions that must be satisfied before they will fund the loan.

Once all conditions are met and the lender is satisfied, the loan will be funded and the money is wired. At this time, if you have not already done so, your down payment is also wired. Upon receipt of all monies, escrow will arrange for the title insurance company to have the sale recorded. Once you have confirmation of recording, it's time to break out the champagne. Congratulations! You just became a homeowner!

SAVVY SHOPPER TIPS: Make sure you understand and agree with all the terms of your loan before loan docs are drawn. Wire the balance of your down payment to escrow two business days before closing to ensure that closing is not delayed. If paying by check, make sure to deposit well in advance in order to allow time to clear. When reviewing the loan documents, the promissory note, and the deed, make sure your name and the property address are spelled correctly. Also, ask that your loan officer be available to accept your phone call in case you have questions during signing.

# CHAPTER 20
## COUNTDOWN TO CLOSING

You're almost there! In just a few days, you'll own your new home! Here are a few things to take care of during this exciting week:

- Sign loan docs and deposit the balance of your down payment to escrow.

- With your agent, do a final walk-through on the property. The purpose of this walk-through is to determine that the property is in relatively the same condition as when you viewed it previously. Specifically, you want to make sure there has been no vandalism, and if the seller has agreed to make repairs, they have been satisfactorily completed.

- Arrange to have utilities switched to your name. It is a good idea to coordinate with the seller so there is some overlap and no chance that you might be without services. In addition to energy utilities, water, and cable, make sure you find out about trash collection. In some areas, it is managed by the city, while in others, there are private companies who provide collection services.

- Submit a change of address to the post office.

- Make arrangements for any cleaning or painting or other projects you want to complete prior to moving in.

- If moving in soon, confirm with your moving company or truck rental agency.

- Make arrangements with your agent to collect your keys and any "clickers" (garage openers, etc.) after closing.

- Although not as time sensitive, many buyers forget to notify various agencies of their move. Remember to update your voter registration, notify the Department of Motor Vehicles of your address change, and provide your new address to your auto insurance agent. A change of location may mean an adjustment in rate.

If you're buying a brand new home, the builder's representative will supply you with all the answers to any of your questions, along with warranties and manuals. If you're buying a foreclosure, you're on your own in terms of learning about the property and how everything works. On the other hand, if buying from a seller who occupied the property, try to have them meet you for your walk-through, or email them your questions. Here are some suggested questions:

- Are there manuals and/or warranties for the appliances?

- Is there a warranty from the builder or a separate warranty for the roof?

- If there is a security system, which company provides the monitoring, what does it cost, and how does it work?

- Where is the mailbox? Is there a key?

- If there is an automatic landscape sprinkler system, are there instructions for setting the controls?

- When was the last time any of the chimneys were cleaned (if wood burning)?

- Where are the exterior clean-outs for the drains?

- If on a septic system, it was probably inspected. Make sure you know where the tank is located and how it is accessed.

- Are the property lines clearly marked?

- Where is the main shut-off for the water and gas?

- Swimming pool or spa? Have the current owner walk you through basic operations.

- Learn how to operate any exterior lights, fountains, or ponds.

- Is there any type of built-in water softener or filter? How does it operate?

- When was the last time the furnace filter was changed?

- Who are the current service providers (gardener, pool maintenance, etc.), and what are their phone numbers?

Every home is different, and the questions you need to ask will vary according to the type and age of your home and where you live. But do take time to ask your questions now while you and your agent still have access to the seller.

SAVVY SHOPPER TIPS: Do not waive the right to a final walk-through. Check the property carefully to make sure the condition is relatively the same as when you last saw it. When meeting with the seller and learning about operating lights, pools, or sprinklers, take notes! You will not remember everything. Keep these notes and any warranty or equipment information in a file folder for easy reference in the future.

# CHAPTER 21
## HAPPILY EVER AFTER
## KEEPING THE ROMANCE
## WITH YOUR HOME ALIVE

Congratulations! You've just purchased a home. Whether this is your starter home, move-up home, forever home, or your downsize home, it is an exciting experience, and a big commitment. Beyond the financial commitment to make payments on your loan, there is also a commitment to take care of the property. Not only is that commitment part of your promise to the lender, it is critical to maintaining and improving the value of your investment.

## Maintaining Your New Home

Unfortunately, some buyers lose their enthusiasm once they realize there is no landlord to call, and small repairs and mowing the lawn starts to eat up their weekends. At the other end of the spectrum, there are those who are eager to tackle a long list of home improvement projects. Wherever you lie on the home-project scale, here are a few tips that will help you keep the romance with your home alive:

- *Home maintenance is like laundry: If you just keep putting it off, the task becomes overwhelming.* When small problems appear, try to take care of them before they become a major issue. If a faucet has a slight drip, fix it before you waste hundreds of gallons of water. If a storm loosens a fence post, reset it before the next storm takes down the whole fence.

- *Do not attempt DIY projects for which you are not qualified.* One of the quickest ways to ruin the value of your home is to fill it with unprofessional finishes. You can certainly learn, and DIY projects are fun, but do seek advice and start with a project that is manageable, like painting a room or hanging a light fixture, versus adding a tile backsplash or crown molding. And whatever you do, finish it! Nothing is worse than a house full of half-completed projects.

- *If you plan on selling in the next couple of years, try to avoid decorations or improvements that are too taste-specific.* For instance, lining the living room walls with knotty pine for that cabin feel, or hanging zebra-print wallpaper in the guest room, could be a big turn-off for many buyers. If you're planning to stay indefinitely, go for it, and satisfy your inner decorator.

- *Have some money saved for unforeseen repairs,* such as when your dog runs through the screen door or you manage to spill a gallon of paint on the living room carpet. Things happen to homes, and they aren't always covered by insurance or a warranty.

Be proud of your home and respect the money you've invested. Show it some love, and you'll enjoy many years of happy homeownership.

*And speaking of happily ever after, here is a fun little real estate story!*

*Last summer, one of my listings was in escrow, with a very sweet young man as the buyer. The property was a charming townhome—perfect for him, his girlfriend, and their young child. They were so excited when my seller accepted their offer, and couldn't wait to move into their first home!*

*A few days before closing, the buyer made a special request of his agent, who then contacted me, and I confirmed with my seller: The following day, with the seller's permission, he took his sweetheart to the condo and proposed inside the home that they would soon share! Can it get any more romantic? I shed a tear just thinking about it, and of course she said "yes."*

## That Unexpected Property Tax Bill

Sometime around 4–9 months after purchasing your home, you might receive what is called a *supplemental property tax bill*. This will depend on the state and county where you live, so be sure to check with your escrow officer or attorney so you'll be prepared.

In California, property taxes are based on a local tax rate, which is applied to an assessed value. When a property is sold, the sales price becomes the new assessed value until such time as it is re-assessed, due to overall increases or decreases in home values. So, if you buy a home for $700,000 and it was previously assessed at $500,000, your new taxes will be based on the $700,000 sales price.

This doesn't happen instantly, however, so any taxes you pay at closing or any impound account that is set up is based on the current assessed value—in this example, $500,000. As the new assessed value becomes effective the day after closing, you will receive a supplemental bill for the difference between the old tax and the new tax. So, in our example, if you closed escrow on November 1, sometime in the spring of the following year, you would receive a supplemental tax bill on the $200,000 difference between the previous $500,000 assessed value and the new value of $700,000. The bill would cover the time period from November 2—after you closed escrow—through June 30, as the new property tax year begins on July 1. The changes to the regular tax bill will be reflected in the bill you receive in September, and if you have an impound account, that new bill will go directly to your lender. This will mean an increase in your monthly payment to cover the increased taxes.

SAVVY SHOPPER TIPS: Stay on top of home maintenance items. Issues seldom disappear and tend to get larger and more expensive over time. Make sure you have some money tucked away for repair items that aren't covered by insurance or a home warranty. Be prepared for a supplemental tax bill by asking questions and doing your calculations in advance.

# FINAL THOUGHTS

Well, by now you must have figured out that I love real estate and the entire process of buying and selling homes. Real estate today is a rapidly-changing industry, highly impacted by advancing technologies in the areas of document management, marketing, advertising, inspection, and home valuation. But at the heart of the business, it's still all about people and helping them achieve homeownership goals.

My hope is that, over the course of reading this book, you've become a savvy shopper and are less terrified of the home-buying process—and better prepared to get the best possible deal. While it's impossible to cover every conceivable circumstance in one book, I hope that you now know where to turn to get your questions answered if your particular situation wasn't addressed. Or contact me, and I'll do my best to help you find an answer.

If you come away with nothing else, I hope you understand the importance of finding the right agent to represent you in your purchase. Your real estate agent is your champion. They should be ready to strongly negotiate on your behalf and be sympathetic to your concerns. Your personalities should click, and, in the best-case scenario, a bond of trust and friendship will develop.

I'm proud to be a REALTOR, and I like to think I've expanded my reach and helped more people by writing this book. I'd love to hear what you think, so please leave a review or contact me directly with your feedback or questions at *marti@kilby.com*. You can also stay on top of my latest blog posts at *www.steelegrouprealty.com/blog*.

Happy house hunting!
Marti Kilby

# GLOSSARY

Here are a few terms and acronyms used in the book that might need additional explanation:

**1003**

The 10-Oh-3 is the Fannie Mae Uniform Residential Loan Application, which is the standardized form used across the country by mortgage-lending institutions.

**Amortization**

In real estate, amortization most commonly refers to paying off a mortgage by making regular equal payments over the term of the loan. A 30-year fixed-rate mortgage is a fully amortizing loan that is paid off in 30 years by making equal monthly payments.

**CC&Rs**

Covenants, Codes, and Restrictions are rules established by a developer or homeowners' association to govern certain aspects of ownership within a specific development or complex. CC&Rs may place restrictions on paint color, parking, exterior improvements, noise, rentals, and more.

**Comps**

Refers to comparable properties that are most similar to the subject property. Comps are researched in order to determine accurate market value for a given piece of property. Comps that have sold within the last six months are the most valuable.

## Concession

Providing something of value to the other party in a transaction in order to reach an agreement. For example, a seller might offer $5,000 towards the buyer's closing costs, or a buyer might offer to allow the seller to stay rent-free in the property for three days past close of escrow.

## Contingency

A condition of purchase that must be satisfied within a specific time frame once escrow has opened. For instance, in California, the buyer's loan approval contingency must generally be removed within 21 days.

## Convey

Convey means to be included in the sale of the property and usually refers to personal property. For example, a refrigerator is personal property, as it is not attached and therefore may or may not convey with the property.

## EMD

The earnest money deposit or good faith deposit represents the initial deposit a buyer makes on a purchase. It is generally deposited with escrow or with the attorney within three days of a purchase contract being executed by both parties.

## HOA

Acronym for homeowners' association. An HOA is an organization within a development that makes and enforces rules for the homes within its jurisdiction and provides certain common-interest services, such as landscaping or a community pool. Owners are charged a monthly HOA fee, and membership is part of owning in that particular community.

## HVAC
Acronym for heating, ventilation, and air conditioning.

## Mello-Roos
Mello-Roos Community Facilities Districts raise money for facilities and services in California through special taxes. The taxes must be approved by a two-thirds vote of residents of the district and are paid as part of the homeowner's annual property tax. If a home is in a Mello-Roos district, it must be disclosed to the buyer.

## MIP
Acronym for mortgage insurance premium. When you obtain an FHA loan, the FHA assesses an upfront and monthly insurance premium to protect against your default.

## MLS
A multiple listing service is a regional organization that allows brokers to share listing information on an online platform that provides both public and broker-only information.

## Mortgage Interest Deduction
The IRS mortgage interest deduction allows homeowners to deduct the amount of interest they pay on their mortgage against their taxable income, according to IRS guide-

lines.

## PITI

Lenders' acronym for principal, interest, taxes, and insurance—the four possible components of your monthly house payment.

## PMI

Private mortgage insurance is paid by a borrower obtaining conventional financing when the down payment is less than 20%. It is paid on a monthly basis to insure the lender against borrower default. The amount of the monthly premium is determined by the amount of down payment, loan amount, and the borrower's credit score.

## Points

Points are also referred to as discount points. They are paid to the lender to "buy down" or reduce the interest rate. 1 point equals 1% of the loan amount, so $1,000 for every $100,000.

## Reserves

When qualifying for a loan, the lender may want to see proof you have sufficient funds in some type of account to cover 3–6 months of your house payments with taxes and insurance.

## Value Range Pricing

This is a method of pricing a property for sale in a range, such as $571,000-$599,000, instead of a single price, such as $589,000. This may increase the number of people who find the home in an online search.

# APPENDIX

## HOUSE-HUNTING CHECKLIST

There's more to viewing a home than counting the bedrooms and bathrooms! Here are some other important consider-ations that can often be overlooked, especially regarding a home's condition and functionality. Completing a checklist with notes for each home you visit is a good way of determin-ing how well the home would fit your needs and how much work it might need in comparison to other homes you view.

Follow this link or place in your web browser to download a pdf version of the House-Hunting Checklist.

https://pages.convertkit.com/7a496e338a/d7c69acc9e

.................................................. ............................
ADDRESS                                        DATE

☐ Curb appeal / condition of front yard:

..........................................................................................

☐ Condition of other homes on the street:

..........................................................................................

☐ Condition of roof as visible:

..........................................................................................

☐ Condition of exterior walls and trim:

..........................................................................................

☐ Entry foyer / or opens directly into living space:

..........................................................................................

☐ Kitchen work space / storage / layout:

..........................................................................................

☐ Condition of cabinets / appliances:

..........................................................................................

☐ Living room / family room / size / furniture layout:

..............................................................................................................

☐ Child safety / banisters / stairs:

..............................................................................................................

☐ Condition of bathroom(s):

..............................................................................................................

☐ Condition of interior walls and trim:

..............................................................................................................

☐ Condition of flooring:

..............................................................................................................

☐ Condition of window coverings:

..............................................................................................................

☐ Closet space in bedrooms:

..............................................................................................................

☐ Location of laundry:

..............................................................................................................

☐ Overall storage:

.............................................................................................................................

☐ Condition of back yard / patio:

.............................................................................................................................

☐ Noise interior / exterior:

.............................................................................................................................

☐ Condition of windows:

.............................................................................................................................

☐ Garage condition / storage:

.............................................................................................................................

# KNOW YOUR FAIR HOUSING RIGHTS AS A BUYER

As a home buyer, you have the right to purchase the home of your choosing without discrimination or limitations based on your race, sex, color, religion, handicap, familial status, or national origin. In practice, this means you have the right to:

- Be shown a broad selection of homes in your price range without limitation to certain neighborhoods.

- Receive equal professional service by your real estate agent.

- Receive equal consideration for financing and insurance.

- Experience fair appraisal practices.

- Be given reasonable accommodation for persons with disabilities.

- Be free from harassment when exercising your fair housing rights.

These rights are national law under the following:

- Civil Rights Act of 1964

- Fair Housing Act

- Americans with Disabilities Act

- Equal Credit Opportunity Act

Additionally, there may be state and local laws that provide broader coverage in protecting groups not covered by federal law.

If you suspect discrimination, contact your local Board of REALTORS, and/or contact your local office of Housing and Urban Development (HUD) to file a complaint.

With that said, I'd like to share one final story:

> *Several years ago, I was showing a lovely couple a nice home in a well-maintained neighborhood in northern San Diego County. The home needed some updates, but that didn't scare my buyers, as this was the neighborhood they desired. The owner and his wife were there packing and cleaning, as the home had belonged to his recently deceased sister.*

> *My clients stepped out into the back yard to examine the outside area, and the owner bent over and whispered to me in a confidential manner, "You know, there are some other people like them that live at the end of the cul-de-sac, so your buyers wouldn't be alone or feel like they're the first ones in the neighborhood."*

> *OMG! Did he REALLY just say that, or was I flashing back to the 1960s or '50s? I was so taken aback I could barely speak! I gathered my wits, smiled, and simply replied, "My buyers currently live in the neighborhood and are very familiar with it. That is why they are looking here." He just shrugged, and I walked away to join my buyers.*

> *I did not share the exchange with my clients, but I was nervous that the owner would discriminate against my buyers on the basis of race should they de-*

*cide to write an offer. If they did, I felt that I would need to share the conversation with the listing agent and explain my fears, as discrimination is not only against the law, it is a violation of the REALTOR Code of Ethics.*

*In the end, my clients opted for a different home, but I have often wondered what would have happened had they pursued the purchase...*

# BIBLIOGRAPHY

Fidelity National Title. *California Buyer & Seller Guide to Title & Escrow*. Fidelity National Title, 2012. Accessed June 2018. http://zabemortgage.com/wp-content/uploads/2016/04/ ZABE_Fidelity_EscrowBuyerSellerGuide.pdf.

US Tax Center. "7 Things You Should Know About Gift Tax." US Tax Center. October 07, 2014. Accessed June 2018. https://www.irs.com/ articles/7-things-you-should-know-about-gift-tax.

# WHAT PEOPLE
## ARE SAYING

*Marti Kilby provides today's home buyer with a step-by-step guide to buying real estate that is easy to understand, detailed, and comforting. A MUST-READ not only for first-time home buyers, but seasoned veterans as well. Marti's no-nonsense explanation of the process of buying a home, from start to finish, takes all the uncertainties and fears out of the equation. Read this book as you begin your journey of finding the perfect home, and you're sure to have "Home Buying Power."*

*Troy De Mond*
*REALTOR*
*Royal Shell Real Estate, Inc.*
*Fort Myers, FL*

*I just finished reading Marti Kilby's "Home Buying Power." What a fantastic guide for home buyers! It can be a life saver for first-time buyers and a great review for experienced buyers and sellers. This book provides an easy-to-follow explanation of terms and procedures. I love the Savvy Shopper notes at the end of the chapters and the short stories based on her experience. Marti is right on!*

*Barbara Keane*
*REALTOR*
*Berkshire Hathaway HomeServices*
*Palm Springs, CA*

*Before reading Marti's book, "Home Buying Power: the Savvy Shopper's Guide to Paying Less and Getting More in any Real Estate Market," I would've been considered the opposite of savvy. More like woefully uneducated. I heard friends who were buying their first homes using terms like escrow, closing costs, PMI, all sorts of words and acronyms that sounded completely foreign to me. I knew one day I wanted to buy my own home, and in order for that to happen, I needed to be informed. Thanks to Marti and her clear writing and relatable examples, I now feel I can take on the home-buying process with confidence! She walks you through the entire journey, thoroughly explaining each step along the way. I now understand all of the terminology that used to confuse me, and I learned so much more beyond vocabulary. This book not only gave me a better understanding of what to expect when buying a home, it is also a great tool to have with me when the home-buying dream becomes a reality. Marti makes you feel like you have a trusted friend by your side, guiding you to get the most out of your experience. I highly recommend "Home Buying Power" if you want to be fearless and knowledgeable when making what is most likely the biggest investment of your life.*

*Emily Carminati*
*Radio Personality*
*San Diego, CA*

# ABOUT THE AUTHOR

M arti Steele Kilby is broker/owner of Steele Group Realty in La Mesa, California. She has been a REALTOR for over thirteen years and is a Certified Residential Specialist (CRS), with the Residential Real Estate Council. Marti has been recognized for three consecutive years as a Five Star Professional featured in San Diego Magazine.

Prior to her real estate career, Marti specialized in health and fitness marketing and management for industry leaders including the Aerobics & Fitness Association of America (AFAA) and Healthclub.com. When not working or writing, Marti enjoys Zumba, gardening, traveling and enjoying life with her husband and nine grandchildren.

You can follow Marti's real estate blogs at:

*https://activerain.com/blogs/martikilby*

and

*https://www.steelegrouprealty.com/blog*

Made in the USA
San Bernardino, CA
18 January 2019